JOHN RUSSELL TAYLOR

GREAT MOVIE MOMENTS

PHOTOGRAPHS FROM THE KOBAL COLLECTION

Crescent Books
New York

This 1987 edition published by
Crescent Books
Distributed by Crown Publishers, Inc.
225 Park Avenue South
New York, New York 10003

Text copyright © 1987 John Russell Taylor
Picture selection copyright © The Kobal Collection

English titles of foreign language films are given
when the film is commonly known by that title.

Edited by Sarah Bevan
Designed by Paul Bowden

Page one: *Citizen Kane*, 1941
Frontispiece: Harold Lloyd in *Safety Last*, 1923
Above: Anthony Quinn in *Zorba the Greek*, 1964

ISBN-0517-65350-8

Manufactured in Hong Kong

h g f e d c b a

Acknowledgments The publishers would like to thank the following film distribution and production
companies whose publicity film stills appear in this book: Allied Artists, André Paulvé, Avco-
Embassy, CICC, Ciné-Alliance, Cinema-Center, Cineriz, Cocinor-Marceau, Columbia, Constantin
Film, Decla-Bioskop, Ealing, Edison, EMI, Enigma, Epoch, Falcon, Gaumont, Goldwyn Co., Hal
Roach, Handmade, ITC, London Films, Lucasfilm, Lux, Mosfilm, MGM, Nero Film, Omni-Zoetrope,
Paramount, P.E.A., Rank, RKO, Star Film, Svensk Film-industri, Selznick International, Seven Arts,
Tobis, Toho, 20th Century-Fox, Ufa, Unitalia, United Artists, Universal, Warner Bros. And thanks
also to the staff of the National Film Archive Films Stills Dept.

CONTENTS

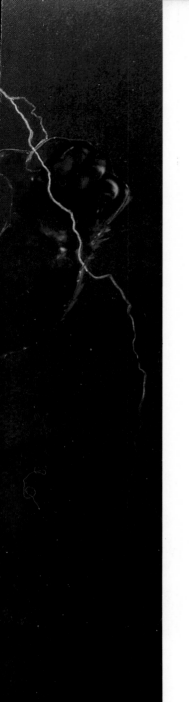

INTRODUCTION

Whichever way you phrase it, it never seems quite right. Memorable Moments from Great Movies? Great Moments from Memorable Movies? Great Images from the Movies? Great Images of the Movies? Images of Great Movies? Each formulation covers most, but none exactly covers all, of what one has in mind. The most obvious objection is the basic one that famous movie stills never correspond precisely with what is actually in the film. At best, they are reconstructions of what appears on screen, or records of what is happening in front of the camera from a rather different angle. And of course frame enlargements from the film itself, though often revealing, are seldom very satisfactory as images in their own right.

But for most of the cinema's history, movie stills and movie portraits have been the only readily accessible reminder of what we have seen, or think we have seen, so that memory can often play tricks on us by moving back into a film a moment that only ever existed as a still. Just as millions are convinced that they have heard Humphrey Bogart say 'Play it again, Sam,' in *Casablanca* or Charles Boyer murmur sexily 'Come wiz me to ze Casbah' in *Algiers*, though the lines were never in fact uttered, so millions believe that they have seen Glenn Ford give Rita Hayworth an almighty side-swipe on the dance-floor in *Gilda* though he never does that either, except in a famous still used in a famous poster. (Enter a further layer of ambiguity: stills were seldom used directly in posters, but merely formed the basis of art-work which could diverge at will even further than the staged still from screen actuality – witness Jane Russell in *The Outlaw*, with a gun or a whip, with or without defined cleavage.)

And yet the movie is undeniably a visual medium, and we recall it visually; that means, as a rule, that we recall it in terms of still images: our memory for movement is always a bit more hazy. (There are certain favourite camera-movements in films which, every time I see them, take me by surprise because they are significantly faster or slower than I remember.) And frequently, to the long list of memories from films we have seen is added a selection of pseudo-memories from films we have not seen, but have often seen illustrated. Sometimes the important sources for these detached images can be readily tracked down to one influential book or another. For a generation senior to mine it seems to have been, as often as not, Paul Rotha's pictorial anthology *Movie Parade*, published by The Studio in 1936 and getting, apparently, to a large new audience which had not up to then had any marked visual interest in films. For me and my generation, I suspect it was Roger Manvell's very influential Pelican *Film*, first published in 1944, revised in 1946 and further revised in 1950.

I find it is amazing how often, when a particular title calls a particular image to mind, that image proves to be the illustration Manvell picked: the two detectives in *Blackmail* with the shadow of the venetian blind across their faces; Falconetti having

Above: **Notorious** *(1946; dir. Alfred Hitchcock). A scene that never was, but which has been endlessly reproduced until everyone believes he has seen it.* Photograph by Ernest Bachrach

Previous page: **King Kong** *(1933). The still on pages 66-7 shows the scene that really appears in the film; this is the publicity photograph. Not a genuine moment, but just as persuasive as an image of the film.* Photograph by Bob Coburn

her hair cut in *La Passion de Jeanne d'Arc*; the 'walls of Jericho' in *It Happened One Night*; the great bearded shadow of *Ivan the Terrible* cast on the wall. And, of course, the woman with the spectacles smashed in her face from the Odessa Steps sequence of *Battleship Potemkin*. But that seems to go even further, as an image which, from whatever source, has entered the universal memory bank, to be constantly quoted by other artists in other media, from Francis Bacon down.

So what, beyond a bit of easy nostalgia, do these images have that makes them stick in the memory? Is it just the visual equivalent of Noël Coward's 'Strange, the potency of cheap music'? (Another line, incidentally, which was never actually said.) Or is there some distinguishing feature? Does the value of the film itself make any difference, or can there be the cinematic equivalent of the one-line poet, like J.W. Burgon, remembered solely (and deservedly) for his description of Petra as 'a rose-red city, half as old as time'? How many of these one-liners, as well as being images in the most literal sense of the term, are also images in a wider, metaphorical sense, gathering within themselves the essence of some human experience – perhaps summing up exactly what we want to remember of a whole film, or reaching deeper into our subconscious to bring to the surface who knows what wonders and mysteries?

Of course it would be simplest if the whole idea could be compressed into one composite notion of Great Stars in Great Moments from Great Movies. But even then, would the images concerned be imagination-grabbing in themselves? Would they necessarily encapsulate the films they illustrate? There is, after all, such diversity in what people remember from movies, and the way they remember it.

Consider for a moment *Casablanca*. To begin with, what immediately conjures it up is not a literal image but a line of dialogue which, as has already been remarked, people only think they have heard anyway. The vagaries of the folk memory being what they are, it is seldom if ever apparent in advance what will emerge as the time-capsule holding a whole movie-experience in suspension. During the shooting of a film where it was undecided almost until the last day which man the heroine would end up with, how could anyone realize that the key moment would be when either Humphrey Bogart or Ingrid Bergman or both say something like 'Play it again, Sam'? As a result, there do not seem to be in existence authentic stills of such a moment. There are stills of the moment in the Paris flashback where Bogart and Bergman are standing, champagne in hand, by the piano at which Dooley Wilson is seated. But it is not *the* moment, in Rick's shadowy Café Américain, in war-shadowed but still neutral Casablanca.

And yet, *Casablanca* is, for an inscrutable combination of reasons, one of the best-known movies of all time. It would be absurd not to include a still from it. But what? Here one can only fall back on the secondary meaning of the word 'image', as much metaphorical as literal. Is there a literal image which, whether it is necessarily the one you would first think of, somehow immediately elicits the right response, encapsulating the film in such a way as to provide a sort of microcosm of the whole? Something which represents the whole movie by a moment? Well, clearly it has to have Bogart and Bergman and Casablanca in it. Who else? Conrad Veidt, Claude Rains, Sydney Greenstreet, Peter Lorre? Yes, if possible. But finally they, and all the political thriller side of the story, are merely what Hitchcock would have called the McGuffin; the essential of the story is the romantic triangle, and the circumstances in which it manifests itself. So, if there is to be a third person, it must be Paul Henreid, and the still has to convey something of the web of secrets which surrounds them. But the more one considers it, the more one wonders who remembers about or cares for Paul Henreid anyway? Who ever did, except as the necessary obstacle in the Bogart/ Bergman romance? Finally, it has just to be the two of them, and the rest of the film can almost go hang.

Thinking along the same lines, how would you encapsulate *Gone With the Wind*? Again, oddly, it is words which first come to mind: 'Fiddle-de-dee'; 'I'll never go hungry again'; 'Frankly, my dear, I don't give a damn.' But these all memorialize happenings which are perhaps not very visually remarkable. We may remember Scarlett saying 'I'll never go hungry again', but do we really want to see a still of Vivien Leigh standing defiantly in a pocket-sized studio set which represents the open sky by a very obvious cyclorama? No doubt some sort of encounter between Scarlett and Rhett is in order, but would a still from that final scene really do the trick all by itself? Unless, of course, you regard the single image entirely in the light of a very well and precisely remembered experience of the film. And if that is the case, almost anything would do.

But then, start at the other end. What single image in *Gone With the Wind* stands out, purely as an image? Surely it must be that at the end of the amazing crane-shot in which Scarlett traverses the enormous open-air hospital of the dying and the dead. Spectacular, certainly, but does it really sum up more than a small part of the film? For me, the image which might capture the most important elements — the period, the ins and outs of the central relationship, the stars looking good and characteristic of themselves — is the moment when Scarlett, or rather Vivien Leigh, bored with formal widowhood, throws back her widow's veil to scandalize the locals by dancing with the sceptical, intrigued Rhett, or rather Clark Gable. It is neither the generally best-remembered moment, nor the most visually striking, but it is undoubtedly the one most charged with significance and potentiality, a pivotal point both in the plot and the development of the two central characters. But then, in the final analysis, the film is a love story, and one comes back inexorably to the definitive clinch of the two principals, in a field after Atlanta.

In a very different register, what do we think of, what do we come to with a sense of recognition, when we approach the Marx Brothers in all their demented glory? There are two images, one general and one very specific. The definitive sequence in a Marx Brothers film would, for most people, be the stateroom sequence in *A Night at the Opera*, where character after character, each bent on his or her own independent line of action, is crowded into an already saturated small space. The stills from that may look a little staged — as they certainly were — but there is no denying their validity as a record of a magic movie moment. But there is something more general, or at any rate diffused. It does not necessarily relate to any outstanding moment in any specific film, but is more in the nature of an ideal image which recurs frequently, with slight variations: the encounter of dignity and impudence represented by the impregnable Margaret Dumont and the irrepressible Groucho. As so often in romantic dramas — and is this not, in its own curious way, a romance? — it is what happens between two people that we remember and want to visualize. Rhett and Scarlett, Groucho and La Dumont, Butch Cassidy and the Sundance Kid, it is the attraction/repulsion, the mutual jockeying for position which provides the necessary tension that brings the relationship vividly to life. And any still which pins down something of that on paper is bound to be a memorable image.

Take another example, *Whatever Happened to Baby Jane?* There are, of course, many literal, specific images in the film that people remember: Joan Crawford and the rat in a dish; Bette Davis all dressed up to sing 'I'm Sending a Letter to Daddy.' But in the more general sense the image of the film must contain the two of them. It was, after all, the idea of these two rival screen goddesses together in one film which was at the heart of the film's creation, and which brought millions into the cinema. One could hardly picture the film without both. The same, in a different way, is true of the films in which Alan Ladd and Veronica Lake or Humphrey Bogart and Lauren Bacall, or Dean Martin and Jerry Lewis co-starred — even though in all cases the individuals involved had potent careers outside the particular teaming. In *Broadway Melody of 1940* it just must be Fred Astaire and Eleanor Powell together, dancing, because this summit conference of hoofers was a once-in-a-lifetime event, with each sparking something special out of the other.

Again, these are great happenings, which provide the *raison d'être* and the memory hook for specific films. In *The Rains Came* (or *The Rains of Ranchipur*, for that matter) it was the rains coming. In *Noah's Ark* it was the flood. In *Samson and Delilah* it was the destruction of the temple. In *A Night to Remember* or *Titanic*, it was the Titanic going down. In *Alexander Nevsky* it was the battle on the ice, in *Chimes at Midnight* the battle in the mud. *The Pride and the Passion* turned on getting a giant gun and *Fitzcarraldo* an Amazon steamer up and over a hill. In *Jezebel* the key happening is the pig-headed insistence of Bette Davis on coming to the débutantes' ball in a sinfully red dress, and that is what is visualized, even though the film was in black-and-white and the dress actually used was allegedly green, because that photographed better. And who can think of DeMille's *Cleopatra* without immediately bringing to mind the cut-off point of the barge scene, where the curtains of the couch drift down and the camera modestly withdraws to show dancing-girls, musicians and long ranks of oarsmen propelling the two lovers towards paradise?

In these cases the event, the place, or even the prop, is a far more potent image than any of the people involved. Sometimes it is a combination of the two. Just imagine Laurel and Hardy or Buster Keaton in the Wild West (in *Go West* and *Way Out West* respectively). Or Bette Davis comically dropped in a bed of cactus (in *The Bride Came C.O.D.*). Or it might be the exceptional thing the star did: 'Garbo Talks', in *Anna Christie*, or 'Garbo Laughs' in *Ninotchka*. For the image could be of something that had no particular significance, plotwise or otherwise, in the individual film in which it appeared, but was a turning point or key moment in that other, larger theatre of which the film-goer cannot but be aware, the career of the star who is always appreciably there behind the role. So Garbo plays comedy, or confirmed lightweights like Jane Wyman or Ray Milland suddenly come out with a heavy drama (in *Johnny Belinda* and *Lost Weekend* respectively) and amaze everyone so much that they win Oscars for it.

It may be noted at this point that not all the films cited are great, or even perhaps very good. This brings us on to another aspect of the question: are we talking about memorable moments from great movies, or great moments from memorable movies, or even perhaps unforgettable moments or stunning images from otherwise lousy movies? Extraordinary how potent cheap music can be? – which is what the Noël Coward character actually says. Undoubtedly it is true that many wholly admirable, loftily ambitious, deeply intelligent movies never quite take hold of the imagination, while there are many uncritical choices which lodge themselves securely in the world's memory. No one would say that *Niagara* was a great film, or even a halfway good film, but there are two unforgettable images associated with it, one which was not (regrettably) in the film, the poster picture of a giant Marilyn Monroe stretched out sensuously right across the top of the falls, and the other, which certainly was, when, wearing the provocative red dress (this time caught in full colour) she wiggles off into the distance, sowing discord and desire as she goes. Nor can we ignore the efficacy of the cult movie, the piece of out-and-out schlock like *Little Shop of Horrors* or *Hercules Unchained* which worms its way into our consciousness and will not be put out. There is, after all, always some reason why certain films out of the mass distinguish themselves in this way, and it nearly always has something to do with an image which speaks: the hungry man-eating plant or the muscles of Steve Reeves. We can deprecate the fact until we are blue in the face, but that changes nothing.

Indeed, it is perfectly possible for one generation's trash to become accepted as the next generation's treasure. Take *King Kong*. There, originally, was a straight exploitation film for you, with no claims to be considered as anything else – except, possibly, on the level of technical skill, and those claims were very soon outdated. And yet, there is no doubt that *King Kong*'s peculiar combination of qualities, its rehandling of one of the eternal myths (Beauty and the Beast) and its now very period brand of naïve technical knowingness, do make it into a classic of film art rather than of film exploitation. Certainly it looks these days a lot more truly creative than a multitude of more pretentious films which loudly proclaimed their artistic qualities and vanished without trace after an initial flurry of critical deference. In any case, whatever else it may or may not be, *King Kong* is a film of great visual images, not in the sense that it lingers on carefully composed beauties, but that its story is told entirely in visual terms, each image saturated with meaning and association. Of course we remember Kong atop the Empire State Building (though in fact it is not quite the Empire State) because that is the climactic image, and also the one most used in publicity through the years, but there are dozens of others jostling in the mind of anybody who has seen the film.

The possibility of an image's being the best remembered because the most frequently reproduced opens up a wholly new perspective. Those who believe that publicity can achieve anything would probably take that for granted, but even there, there must be some reason why one image rather than another is chosen for constant reproduction: it must be as impossible to manufacture a magic movie moment from cold as it is to invent a star unless you have the right material to work on in the first place. If that were not so, all saturation publicity campaigns would be equally successful, and common sense tells us they are not. If publicity and initial expenditure were all, *Howard the Duck* would be the major hit of our time.

But we do certainly have to ask ourselves whether familiarity breeds potency. If our memory needs a hook to hang itself on, the image most frequently presented may well provide that hook. And in a way it does not really matter *why* an image has become fixed in our minds, whether it is an image from a film, or more generally, an image of that film. The important thing is that it is there, immovable, a fact of life. The movies have become the great dream factory of the twentieth century, and though we may try to remember our dreams more accurately, and to work out why we dream what we dream, ultimately the dream is the *donnée*, and all the rest is hypothesis. Why do we respond to these images more vividly and durably than any others? Because, like Everest, they're there. And why are they there? Because we respond, and go on responding. The image bank is inexhaustible, and perhaps, rather than questioning, we should just accept and enjoy.

Opposite: **The Battleship Potemkin** *(1925; dir. Sergei Mikhailovich Eisenstein). One of the most famous films ever made. The image of the woman with her spectacles smashed in her eye has turned up so often in painting and print-making that she must by now have entered the collective unconscious.*

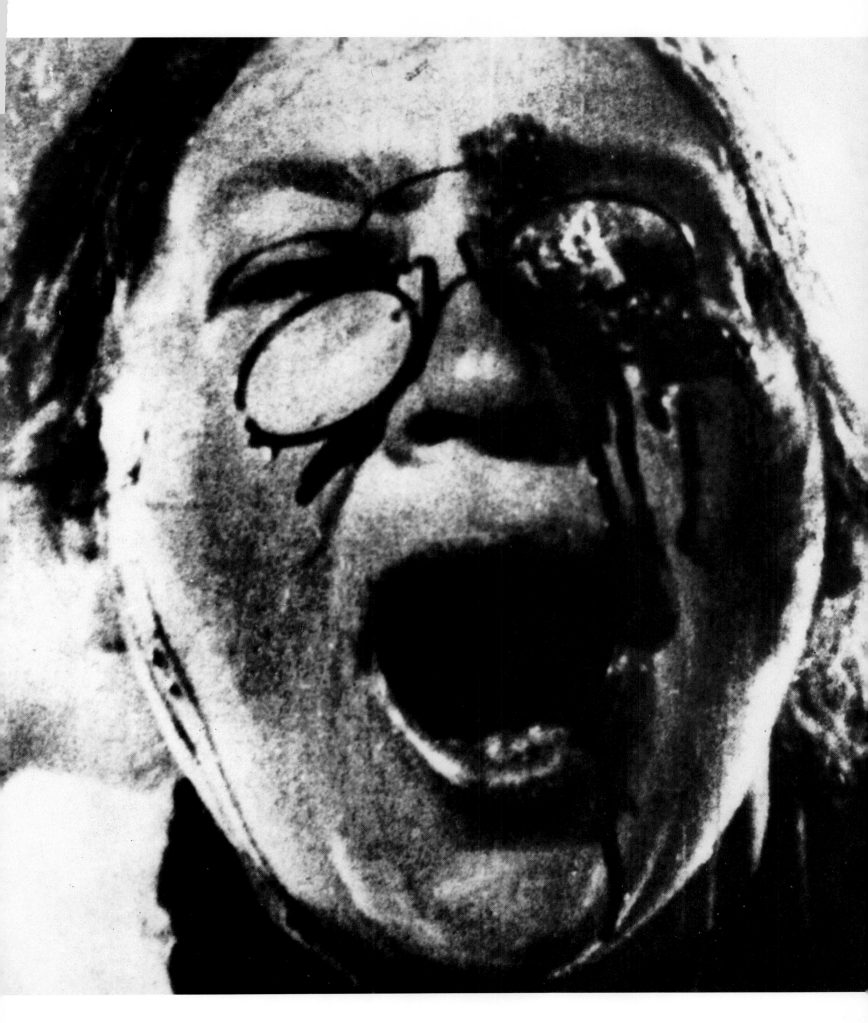

THRILLERS

CRIMES AND PUNISHMENTS

◁ ANGELS WITH DIRTY FACES (1938)
Dir. Michael Curtiz

This is actually a quite stickily moral piece, in which the gangster hero/villain (James Cagney, naturally) is admired and emulated by a group of slum lads (soon institutionalized into the Dead End Kids), but elects eventually to pretend to be a coward when he goes to the electric chair, so that they will be disillusioned and not follow in his footsteps. Here he is preparing to go to his doom, clear-eyed and conscious of having done right at the last.

▽ DOUBLE INDEMNITY (1944)
Dir. Billy Wilder

If she wanted to turn on the heat, no one could do it half so well as Barbara Stanwyck. Here she is, flashing her legs to subjugate easy-going insurance man Fred MacMurray and entice him into murder for love, and money. Again, as in so many James M. Cain stories of wrong-doing in Southern California, it is a husband–wife–lover triangle which leads on to disaster. With Raymond Chandler scriptwriting and Billy Wilder directing, there was plenty of talent around, but as soon as Stanwyck slunk down the stairs in her blonded bangs and high-heeled ankle-straps, no one else in sight got a look-in.

▷ THE POSTMAN ALWAYS RINGS TWICE (1946)
Dir. Tay Garnett

The look of complicity tells it all: in the grips of overwhelming passion and an overwhelming desire (on her part) for upward mobility, a wife (Lana Turner) and her lover (John Garfield) plot and execute the murder of her husband, the boorish owner of a wayside café. Garfield's injury in the otherwise fatal car crash is part of the cover. In this version of James M. Cain's dark tale of crime and punishment, the sex was all unstated, but sizzling; in the eighties remake everything is spelt out, but nothing works half so well, owing to a fatal lack of chemistry between Jack Nicholson and Jessica Lange.

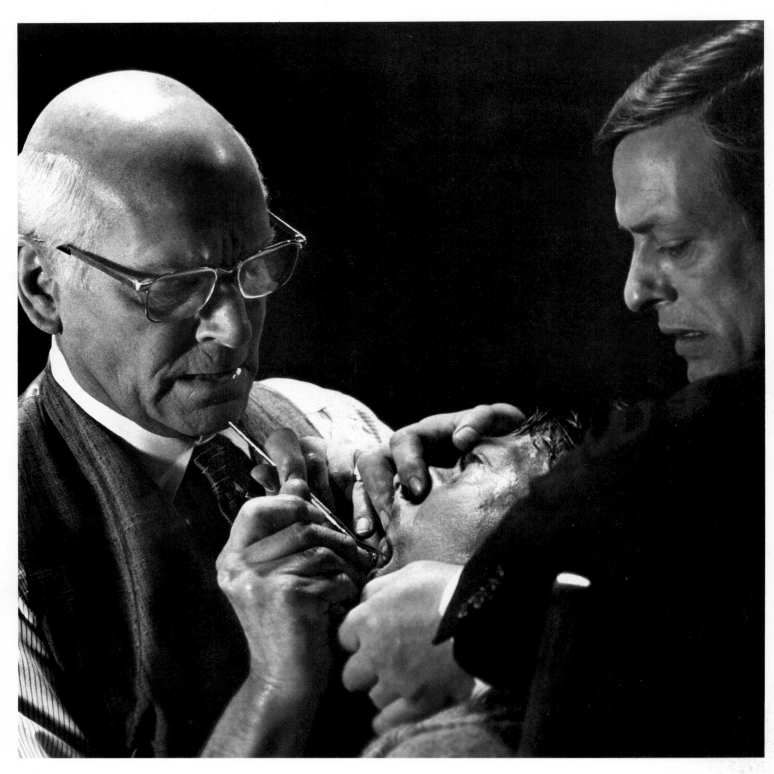

△

MARATHON MAN (1976)
Dir. John Schlesinger

Most people's height of everyday horror would be to be caught in a dentist's chair by a sadistic dentist. But when the dentist is not only sadistic in one's own fantasy, but an ex-Nazi out to hurt you, then horror is compounded a hundredfold. That is the agonizing plight of our hero (Dustin Hoffman), the lone Jewish student who pits himself against the New York Nazis, vigilante-style, and finds himself at the wrong end of Laurence Olivier's drill in consequence. *Photograph by Peter Sorel*

△

THE WAGES OF FEAR/La Salaire de la Peur (1953)

Dir. Henri-George Clouzot

Most relentlessly insistent of on-the-road melodramas, chronicling the endless trials of a group of four Europeans who will do anything to get out of a putrefying Latin American village – even drive two trucks loaded with nitro-glycerine 300 miles over some of the roughest roads in the world. No good comes to anyone in the end, even after all the dangers and disasters which they manage to survive, including having to run over the legs of one of their number (Charles Vanel) when unable to stop in a pool of leaking oil, and having their cargo shaken again and again to the verge of explosion. It was the first French movie in French a lot of English-speakers ever saw.

△
THE MALTESE FALCON (1941)
Dir. John Huston

Maybe the falcon itself is what the plot of John Huston's classic private-eye thriller is all about, or maybe it is just a monumental example of what Hitchcock called the McGuffin – the thing everyone in the film is intensely worried about, though nobody watching it could care less. Whichever way you look at it, the quest for the fabulous bird and its valuable secret gets a lot of extraordinary people very excited. Here the object has finally turned up, and Humphrey Bogart (Sam Spade, private eye) is involved with three shady characters (Peter Lorre, Mary Astor, Sidney Greenstreet) who give it hungry looks and try to decide how they can get it all to themselves. Nobody wins. *Photograph by Mack Elliott*

△

THE THIRD MAN (1949)
Dir. Carol Reed

Though he is on screen for less than twelve minutes, Orson Welles, the 'third man' himself, alias Harry Lime, is what everyone remembers from Carol Reed's (and Graham Greene's) melancholy thriller set in the shadowy ruins of occupied Vienna. His first appearance, a flash in the darkness as a light from an upstairs window briefly stabs the night; his inimitable delivery on the Ferris wheel of the famous line about Switzerland and the cuckoo clocks; and above all his end, caught like a rat in the glistening sewers. The rest of the film was equally distinguished, but the wind of memory bloweth where it listeth.

△ FOREIGN CORRESPONDENT (1940)
Dir. Alfred Hitchcock

Foreign correspondent Joel McCrea is right at the beginning of his eye-opening experiences of fascism in action (not a very comfortable place to be, either in the film or in a Hollywood still constrained by America's neutrality laws), when a leading statesman is assassinated before his eyes on a flight of steps in rainy Amsterdam. A screen full of umbrellas was one of the images Hitchcock had in mind even before he got the plot straight. Others were windmills turning mysteriously the wrong way, and a murder attempt on the top of Westminster Cathedral – the Catholic one, significantly for Jesuit-educated Hitch.

▷ THE ROARING TWENTIES (1939)
Dir. Raoul Walsh

Slum kids James Cagney and Humphrey Bogart go through World War I together then, as 'forgotten men' or something of the sort, get involved in racketeering. Nobody gets much fun out of it all – not even audiences, who by 1939 had seen it all before – but Raoul Walsh kept it all zipping along brightly enough, with a lot of snap and snarl and action highlights. In this sort of fatalistic story, where Cagney in particular is more or less forced into a life of crime, it is all bound to end in death, which finds Cagney this time on a flight of snowy steps, tended only by Hollywood's favourite hooker, Gladys George. *Photograph by Mack Elliott*

△
LAURA (1944)
Dir. Otto Preminger

'That was Laura, but she's only a dream,' crooned the title song. In Otto Preminger's *film noir*, Laura is first a dream, born in the mind of detective Dana Andrews from mooning over the portrait of a vanished girl, then, when she returns unannounced (here, played by Gene Tierney) an uncomfortable reality. The world of the film is picturesquely corrupt, and governed by strange, perverse passions. But that is just as it should be in a film which, almost single-handed, created a mood and a style Hollywood (especially *émigré* Hollywood) was to follow for years.

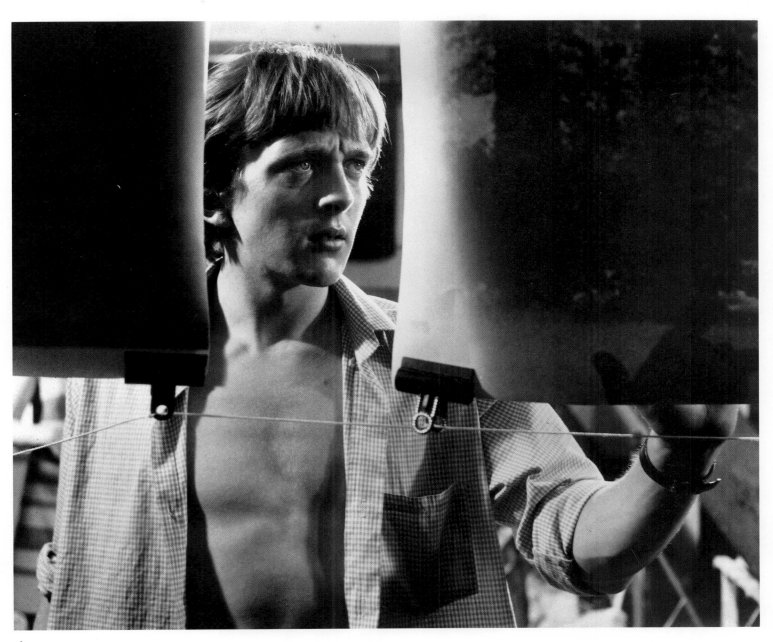

△
BLOW-UP (1966)
Dir. Michelangelo Antonioni

The camera cannot lie – or can it? When London photographer David Hemmings takes some innocent pictures in a deserted park, he never imagines that he may have visual evidence of a shooting. But as he blows the pictures up larger and larger, the evidence gets at once more difficult to ignore and more impossible to define. All part of director Antonioni's play with reality and illusion, of course. But, hitting precisely the tone of the times, his first English-speaking production was a surprise hit and made philosophers of us all.

◁ NORTH BY NORTHWEST (1959)
Dir. Alfred Hitchcock

Hitchcock was a graphic designer and art director by training, so it is not surprising that his films are so rich in unforgettable images. One of the most famous is this sequence from *North by Northwest*, in which Cary Grant, victim of mistaken identity, is left all alone in a desert waste, with just a distant crop-spraying plane. What could be more innocent and harmless than that? As it turns out, in Hitchcock's sinisterly deceptive world, almost anything: things that go bump in the night are generally much less dangerous than things that swoop down during the day, out of a clear blue sky.

△ QUAI DES BRUMES (1938)
Dir. Marcel Carné

If the criminal heroes of Hollywood were fated in the thirties, those of France were much more so. It would be hard to keep a tally of the films in which Jean Gabin ended by being shot down in one of Alexandre Trauner's meticulously-cobbled studio street-sets. The most memorable, and most savagely derided by the post-war New Wave of French cinema, were those written by Jacques Prévert and directed by Marcel Carné. In *Quai des Brumes* Gabin plays a soldier on the run from the service, who turns aside for an overshadowed romance with a beautiful waif (Michèle Morgan) and gets shot down by one of her less savoury contacts before he can reach the safety of a boat.

△
THE PUBLIC ENEMY (1931)
Dir. William Wellman

James Cagney's start in a profitable life of crime, as the feisty little villain you just love to hate. In *The Public Enemy* he smashed his way into screen legend, and the hearts of millions, when he squashed a breakfast grapefruit into the face of too-garrulous girlfriend Mae Clarke. Evidently it was not the way most movie-goers ever did behave, but it seemed to tap some secret desire in the subconscious of millions, and Cagney was never afterwards allowed to forget it.

△

SCARLET STREET (1945)
Dir. Fritz Lang

'You're a painter – paint these!' Thus does *femme fatale* Joan Bennett assert her domination over her harmless cashier lover (Edward G. Robinson) in one of Fritz Lang's best American films – a ruthless tale remade from Jean Renoir's *La Chienne*. The point of the instruction is that Robinson is an unknown Sunday painter of genius, and Bennett is passing off his work as her own – with a nice line in smart talk and seductive glances for the idiot critics. Inevitably it all leads to degradation and death, since this was the heyday of the Hollywood *film noir*, and Lang one of its most brilliant exponents.

◁ SUDDEN FEAR (1952)
Dir. David Miller

When Joan Crawford was not trampling over anyone, male or female, in her determination to get to the right side of the tracks, she was very good at suffering spectacularly – usually menaced in mink. *Sudden Fear* enabled her to have it both ways: a rich woman with a young and virile husband (Jack Palance), she finds that he is plotting with his girlfriend (Gloria Grahame) to get rid of her. Shock. Horror. And a healthy determination grows to fight the would-be killers with their own weapons. They little know whom they have undertaken to terrorize. . . .

▷ UNDERWORLD USA (1960)
Dir. Sam Fuller

In their day, in the fifties and early sixties, Sam Fuller's films were considered extremely violent, and *Underworld USA*, a sort of precursor of the recent urban-vigilante cycle, was widely said to be his most brutal film ever. 'Every shot is a smack in the eye', observed one contemporary commentator gleefully. Most of the violence in this story of a young hoodlum exacting savage revenge for the killing of his father was quite clearly spelt out, but sometimes, as in this moment from the beating-to-death of the father, Fuller found it more effective to leave something to the spectator's imagination.

△

GUN CRAZY (1950)
Dir. Joseph H. Lewis

For many the ultimate cult B-movie, *Gun Crazy* is a low-budget but inventive variation on the Bonnie and Clyde story, about a boy and a girl (John Dall and young British import Peggy Cummins) who just go on a cross-country rampage, determined to get what they want at gunpoint and, if necessary, over the dead body of anyone who stands in their way. As can be seen here, the girl is the more bloodthirsty of the two. Joseph H. Lewis directed with maximum feeling for the gritty reality of the five-and-dime and the corner drugstore in an America God and government forgot.

△

THE LETTER (1940)
Dir. William Wyler

A fine way to start a film: Bette Davis with a smoking gun on the verandah of some steamy colonial bungalow. But then what do you do as a follow-up? What actually follows is a cunning piece of emotional blackmail and double-cross (devised by W. Somerset Maugham and tautly filmed by William Wyler) to ensure it shall never emerge that the man she shot was in fact her lover. But the Orient (very much with a capital 'O') has its own ways of exacting retribution. A fine display of scenery-chewing by Ms Davis, for once under firm control. *Photograph by Bert Six*

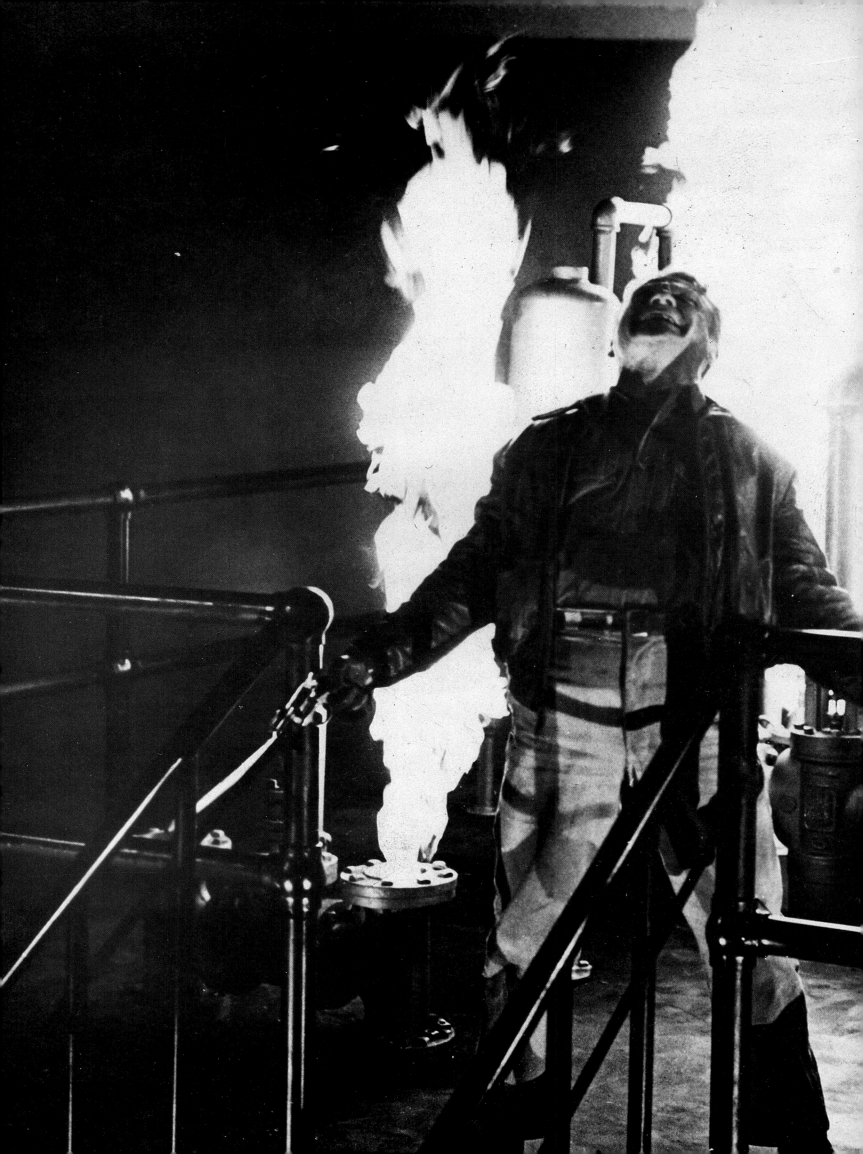

WHITE HEAT (1949)
Dir. Raoul Walsh

'On top of the world, ma, on top of the world!' James Cagney achieves a fiery apotheosis when he deliberately ignites a whole field of giant oil-tanks, going to join the dreadful old mother who has always master-minded his career as a gangster, and whose death while he is in prison has unleashed his final rampage. This was the last and most bizarre of Cagney's classic gangster roles, and carried him off in style to a more benign old age on screen, and then a happy retirement.

SCIENCE FICTION AND FANTASY

THE TIME MACHINE

◁ A TRIP TO THE MOON/Le Voyage dans la Lune (1902)
Dir. Georges Méliès

When Méliès sent his unlikely team of bearded scientists and weirdos off to conquer the moon, obviously the Man in the Moon was bound to take a beating. Méliès was a theatrical magician before he discovered a whole new box of tricks in the cinema, and his fantasy films used to the utmost all the techniques to deceive the eye he could import from the theatre, plus a few that only the camera could encompass. We may laugh appreciatively at the naïve charm of his inventions, but a quick look at later films like *When Worlds Collide* (page 45) suggest that the cinema did not progress all that far in the next fifty years.

△

CLOSE ENCOUNTERS OF THE THIRD KIND (1977)
Dir. Steven Spielberg

Spielberg's *Close Encounters*, however he might edit and re-edit it, always seemed rather like a great beginning and a great ending, with nothing much in the middle. The beginning sees a number of apparently unconnected people having interesting and curious experiences with UFOs. The one who seems to know (or feel) most about them is Richard Dreyfuss, who works for the power company and keeps having unaccountable visions of a mountain. The mountain proves at the end of the film to be the place chosen for the first maximum-publicity, media-covered landing of a giant UFO and the return (unharmed) of the humans who have been spirited away in the past. Special effects and emotional effect overpowering.

▷

IT CAME FROM OUTER SPACE (1953)
Dir. Jack Arnold

. . . And nestled there pulsating, meaning no good to man or beast – or so benighted humanity inevitably supposes. Only wise scientist Richard Carlson recognizes that the aliens have simply made a crash landing on earth, and want nothing better than to repair their meteorite-like spaceship and head back to the stars. His task is complicated by the invisibility of the aliens, except in the zombie-like form of 'doubles' of the local inhabitants which they must create to function on earth. However, in the end they go their peaceful way, the originals of the clones are restored to circulation, and everything goes back to normal, at least until the next time.

◁ WAR OF THE WORLDS (1953)
Dir. Byron Haskin

H. G. Wells saw an invasion from outer space happening in Edwardian London, with knickerbockered cyclists pedalling wildly away across Hampstead Heath. George Pal for the film version imagined it happening, rather, in contemporary Los Angeles, where amphibious-looking spaceships could fight to their hearts' content over Downtown L.A. and demolish City Hall – at that time easily the tallest building in the area. Somehow it survived this early fifties onslaught, to suffer the worse indignity of being dwarfed by its present surroundings.

▽ THINGS TO COME (1936)
Dir. William Cameron Menzies

The rocket has been fired into space, and the fathers of its two occupants philosophize: 'For man, no rest and no ending. He must go on – conquest beyond conquest. . . . And when he has conquered all the deeps of space and all the mysteries of time – still he will be beginning.' H. G. Wells's vision of the future at its most optimistic, but perhaps remembered less for its message than for its gleaming Art Deco sets, courtesy of Vincent Korda and designer-turned-director Menzies.

2001: A SPACE ODYSSEY (1968) ▷▷
Dir. Stanley Kubrick

Stanley Kubrick's 'Space Odyssey' carries mankind from a world not so unlike our own, through the star gate and into another dimension. Most memorable moments: the beginning, where monkeys learn to use weapons through a black basalt teaching machine from outer space; the prolonged battle of wits between the astronauts and the malign computer Hal, who has learnt to think for himself; and the final passage to rebirth through the star gate, which here dazzles astronaut Keir Dullea.

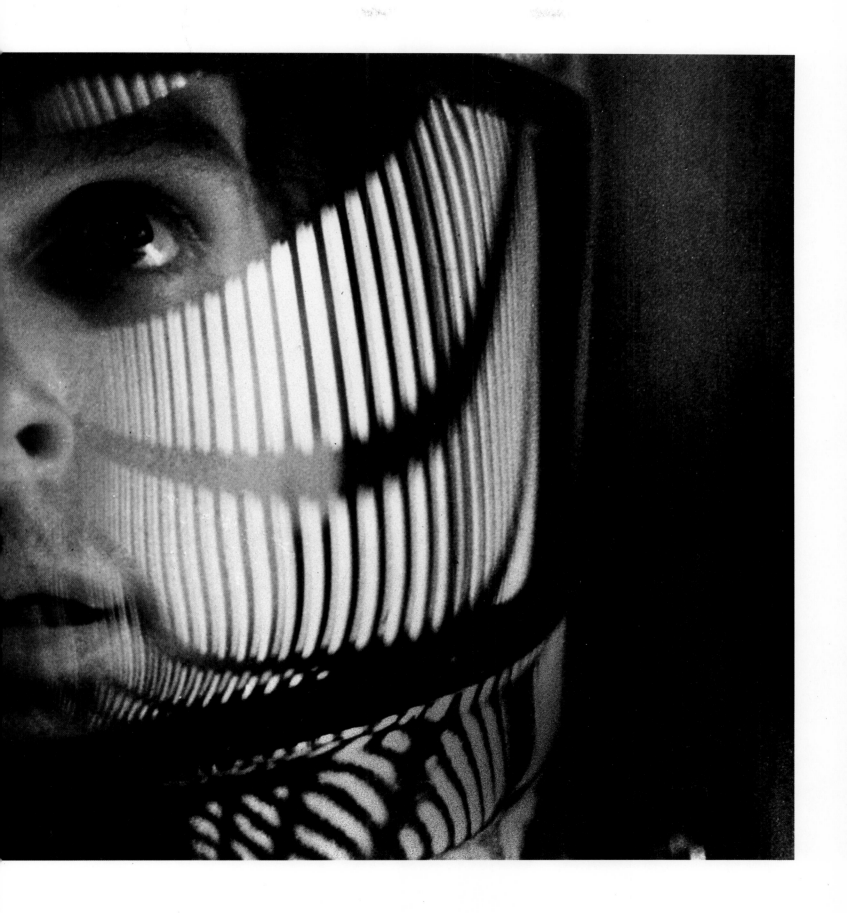

◁

E.T. THE EXTRA TERRESTRIAL (1982)
Dir. Steven Spielberg

When Steven Spielberg announced his intention of filming *Peter Pan*, many critics wondered why he wanted to: had he not already done it in *E.T.*? There are certainly a lot of superficial parallels between Barrie's story of a boy who could never grow up but makes occasional contacts with ordinary humanity, and Spielberg's tale of a small extra-terrestrial somehow left behind after an earth-landing and his relationship with a fatherless earthboy. Towards the end, as the forces of the materialist world close in, E.T. seems to become Tinkerbell, saved from death by the sheer force of the children's desire that he should continue to live. Once that has been achieved, it only remains to get him back to a waiting spaceship, by flying him up into the night on the handlebar of a bicycle.

▽

WHEN WORLDS COLLIDE (1951)
Dir. Rudolph Maté

If worlds are going to collide, it is best if there is plenty of warning: it makes for better effects of panic and destruction, and does enable at least some of the Earth's inhabitants to plan for survival and perhaps a better future elsewhere. In George Pal's skimpy but inventive production there was a lot of play with stock shots of tidal waves, volcanic eruptions and the like before the small group of the chosen (by lottery) could make their escape in a sort of space rocket-cum-Noah's Ark. All done with models and painted backdrops, of course, but designer Charles Bonestall's vision of an Earth in trauma and the brave new world of Planet Zyra was occasionally impressive.

△

STAR WARS (1977)
Dir. George Lucas

If the Force is with you, who or what can be against you? Well, Darth Vader can for one – even if behind the mask and the voice-box there may be a potentially caring, disillusioned human being, sort of. In the intricate inter-galactic world created by George Lucas in *Star Wars* and its two sequels *The Empire Strikes Back* and *Return of the Jedi*, it is difficult to work out precisely to what breed any individual belongs. But probably a number of spectators began to suspect before instalment three that Darth Vader, the dark antagonist of Alec Guinness's saintly Ben Konobi (young Luke Skywalker's spiritual father), might in fact be Luke's real father. (David Prowse, who plays Darth Vader, is in fact never seen full-face, and is heard only with his voice computer-distorted.) Towards the end of the trilogy's first segment, the two father-figures fight it out. *Photograph by John Jay*

△

THE SEVENTH SEAL/Det Sjunde Inseglet (1957)

Dir. Ingmar Bergman

The Knight plays chess with Death for the right to survive. In Ingmar Bergman's grim medieval morality, death is a foregone conclusion for everybody. The Knight (Max von Sydow) and his squire traverse a nightmare world of plague, torture and fanaticism, occasionally lit up by a glimpse of love and beauty. And in the end Death (Bengt Ekerot) claims all, as he leads their dance over the hill and into oblivion.

▽ METROPOLIS (1927)
Dir. Fritz Lang

In Fritz Lang's silent German dream (or sometimes nightmare) of the distant future, the rulers of the great city Metropolis live up aloft in the sunlight, among the skyscrapers and hanging gardens, while the downtrodden workers trudge round, heads bowed, in the underground warrens where the giant machines keep the city turning. Inspired by a beatific vision of the workers' Joan of Arc, Maria, the only son of the city's ruler goes down into the depths to see for himself and share the workers' lot. What he sees there is unforgettable. The film continued to capture imagination in the eighties, with the help of Giorgio Moroder's rock score and some discreet tinting. *Photograph by Horst van Harbov*

▷
THE DAY THE EARTH STOOD STILL (1951)
Dir. Robert Wise

The three leading characters in *The Day the Earth Stood Still*, here rather improbably assembled on the steps of a cardboard spaceship in order that Patricia Neal may be released from her imprisonment within it, are Gort, a robot from outer space who can turn homicidal when roused (for example, by the murder of his master), Neal as the principal genuine human in sight, and Michael Rennie as a statesman-prophet from space called Klaatu, who comes to earth to put human affairs to rights and find out what makes mankind tick. (He does that by lodging with Neal and her young son.) He gets killed for his pains, but fortunately can resurrect in time to stop Gort running amok with the magic phrase 'Gort! Klaatu barada nikto'.

△

THE INCREDIBLE SHRINKING MAN (1957)
Dir. Jack Arnold

A science fiction story that begins with everyday horror and ends with metaphysics. When hero Grant Williams is subjected to radiation he begins unaccountably to get smaller and smaller. As he does so, his predicament is at first slightly comical, then increasingly dis-turbing as he becomes an alien to his (originally) loving and concerned family, and finally gets so small that he is stalked like a mouse by his own friendly domestic pussy and has to fight off a spider with a needle. At the last, he comes in some way to accept his destiny, and sets off into the uncharted thickets of his own front lawn, becoming the first explorer of inner space.

▷

LA BELLE ET LA BÊTE (1946)
Dir. Jean Cocteau

Jean Cocteau retells the classic fairy story with all the romantic fantasy designer Georges Wakhevitch could contrive. The surreal décor of the rich Beast's mansion, with its can-delabra supported by living, moving human arms, fired the imagination of a whole gener-ation, and largely made up for the last-minute deception when the beautiful cat-like Beast dwindles suddenly, redeemed by self-sacrificing love, into the pettish prettiness of Jean Mar-ais. *Photograph by G.K. Aldo*

◁ THE THIEF OF BAGDAD (1940)
Dir. Michael Powell, Ludwig Berger, Tim Whelan

Most memorable of a hundred memorable scenes: the evil vizir Japhar (Conrad Veidt) is instructing his Silver Maid, an alluring automaton (played by Mary Morris) with several supernumerary arms, on how to murder the gullible caliph. Elsewhere we see Japhar summoning up a storm, the thief (Sabu) riding to the Roof of the World on a genie's shoulder, the beautiful princess (June Duprez) breathing in the treacherous odours of the Blue Rose of Forgetfulness, and hero and heroine strung up to await the Death of a Thousand Cuts. By and large, the most successful fairytale in the history of the cinema.

△
SOLARIS (1972)
Dir. Andrei Tarkovsky

Tarkovsky's version of Stanislaw Lem's novel seems almost deliberately to challenge 2001 (page 41), released three years earlier. The Russian film is in grainy black-and-white, and has almost as little coherent plot. It appears that something odd is happening on the distant planet of Solaris, and a psychologist (Donatas Banionis) is sent out to investigate. But as he travels there his own reactions become more confused and subjective. He roams round the cavernous space capsule, preparing (though he does not know it) to meet the mirror of his own psyche, obligingly provided by the planet, which can materialize visitors' obsessions and turn his idyllic dreams of earth into compelling reality.

◁ **SCANNERS** (1980)
Dir. David Cronenberg

Scanners are human beings (either very good or very bad) who have been endowed by some feckless genetic engineering with a special faculty to look into another person's nervous system and telepathically calm or wreak havoc with it. The hero (Stephen Lack) in David Cronenberg's pyrotechnic horror/science fiction fantasy is one of the original guinea-pigs, and at first falls among the bad scanners before he realizes that his power-crazed brother is one of them and must be stopped. There are few more effective ways of stopping someone than by telekinetically exploding his head, though when you have done that at the beginning of the movie what can you do to cap it?

△
THE COMPANY OF WOLVES (1985)
Dir. Neil Jordan

Angela Carter's nasty fairytales for grown-ups usually have a strong sexual undercurrent at least. In collaboration with Neil Jordan she wove three of them into a complex allegory of the onset of puberty in a young girl, the wolves that haunt her dreams standing in for the menacing, unknown country of adult sexuality. The film was a deliberate revival of studio-shooting in elaborately artificial sets (a tribute to Michael Powell), and the special effects department excelled themselves in the transformations of man into wolf.

HORROR

I WAKE UP SCREAMING

◁ **DRACULA** (1931)
Dir. Tod Browning

When people see the original talkie (all-too-talkie) *Dracula* they are usually disap-pointed. Is this rather stolid adaptation of a melodramatic stage hit really the film that chilled a generation? (It was many years later that film-makers thought of going back to the original novel.) Compared with James Whale's contemporary *Frankenstein*, Browning's *Dracula* is decidedly a period piece. And yet, for all its camp, Bela Lugosi's creation as the Transylvanian count who only goes out at night and doesn't 'drink . . . wine' does still afford a *frisson* or two to justify its fame.

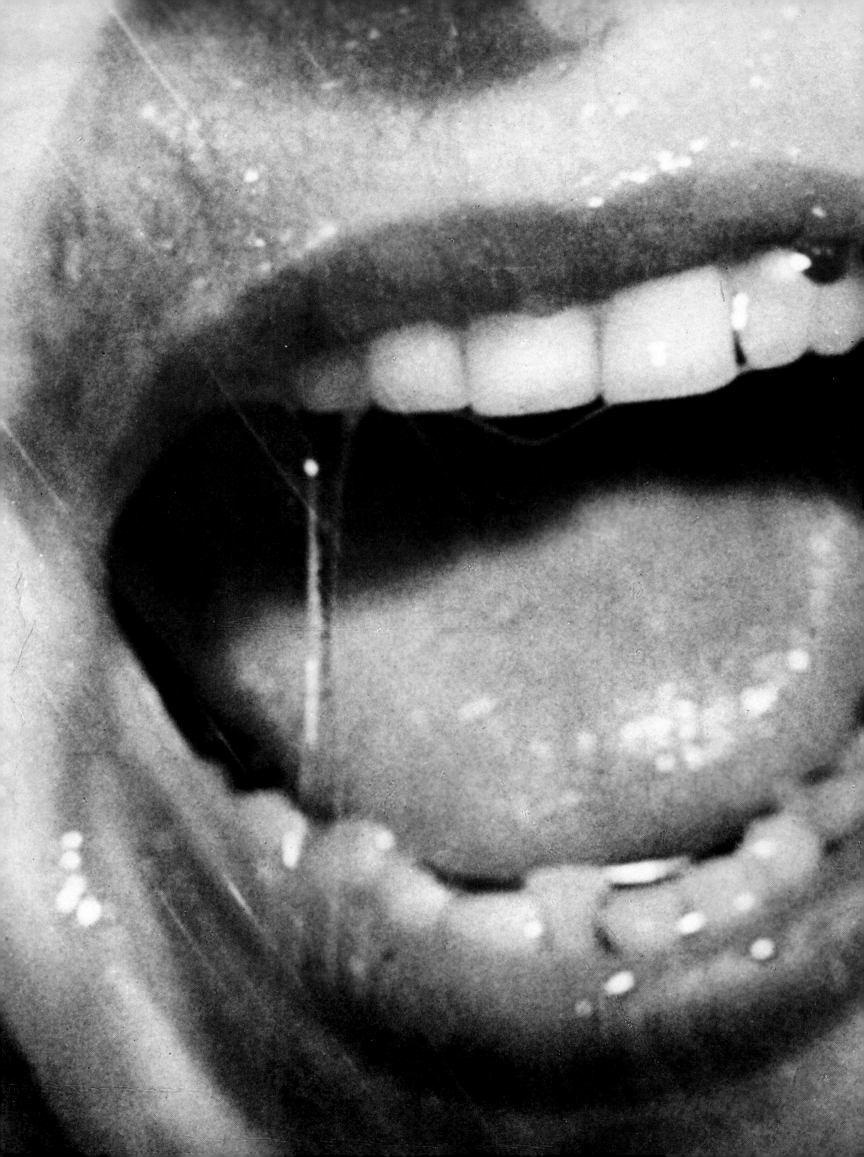

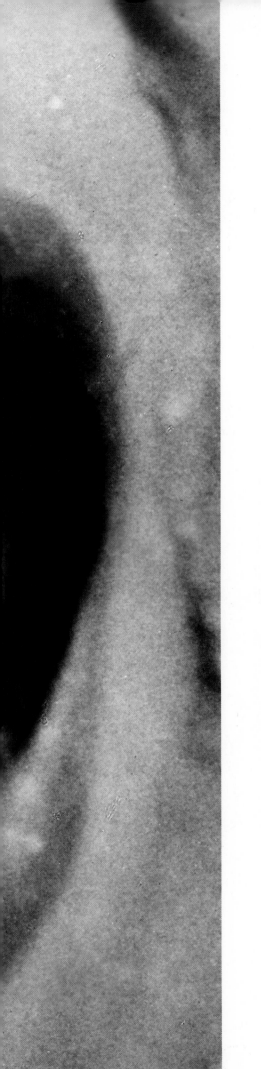

△
◁ **PSYCHO** (1960)
Dir. Alfred Hitchcock

Everyone remembers the house – now religiously re-erected as the prime sight on Universal's studio ride – and the shower scene in which Janet Leigh is so brusquely disposed of by Norman Bates, or Norman Bates's mother, or both. As Norman, Anthony Perkins presents an outline almost as instantly recognizable as the house in which he lives . . . alone. And Janet Leigh's bloody demise was quite so shocking not only because of Hitchcock's callous brilliance in the *mise-en-scène*, but also because nobody, but nobody, kills a heroine halfway through a film.

HALLOWEEN (1978)
Dir. John Carpenter

When John Carpenter made a low-budget but fairly stylish horror thriller called *Halloween* no one could have guessed the amazing number of sequels and spin-offs it would lead to. But the mad killer of young girls, vengefully escaped from some kind of mental institution, was already showing signs of personal indestructibility which boded well for his future, if not for that of every suburban teenager in sight. And he had the nastiest way of using trick-or-treat disguises for his own ends. . . .

THE EXORCIST (1973)
Dir. William Friedkin

Friedkin's extravagances with *The Exorcist*, building and rebuilding sets until he felt they were just right, became legendary. But so did the box-office returns, which encouraged a spate of subsequent films about demonic possession and the like. Here, in a moment heavy with potentiality, the exorcist himself (Max von Sydow) pauses just outside the house where Linda Blair is going through all the torments of the damned that a fertile special effects department could devise.

◁ THE PHANTOM OF THE OPERA (1943)
Dir. Arthur Lubin

In a memorable silent version Lon Chaney
played the hideously disfigured lurker in
the sewers; in the first of several talkie ver-
sions and variations it was Claude Rains.
Both of them, at the climax of the phantom's campaign to have his protégée
starred at the opera, sawed through the
same chandelier in the same opera-house
set, which is still standing in Universal City.
In the talkie the screams on the sound-
track added an extra dimension of sensational alarm.

▷ FRANKENSTEIN (1931)
Dir. James Whale

Paradoxically, the most famous sequence
from James Whale's *Frankenstein* is one
which hardly anyone has seen in its enti-
rety, since its conclusion – in which Boris
Karloff's monster, with deadly innocence,
throws the friendly little girl into the water
just as she has thrown her flowers – has
nearly always been cut. Pathos or black
humour, who can say? But in its ambiguity
very typical of Whale's sophisticated goth-
ick masterpiece, which defined Karloff for
ever as a horror icon. *Photographs by Sher-
man Clark*

◁

THE SPIRAL STAIRCASE
(1945)
Dir. Robert Siodmak

Robert Siodmak's elegant horror-thriller was one of the classics of the forties *film noir* in Hollywood, using the interiors of the shadowy mansion where most of it takes place to create mystery and menace in the grand old German expressionist fashion. Outside a maniac stalks and kills young women with some sort of physical defect. He must be one of those living in the big house, but which? A tense situation, especially since there is also living there Dorothy McGuire, beautiful but mute. . . .

▷

THE CABINET OF DOCTOR CALIGARI/Das Cabinett des Dr Caligari (1919)
Dir. Robert Wiene

The original idea of Wiene's film was that it should tell its story straight from the fantastic world of German romanticism, full of fiendish doctors, somnambulist slaves controlled by the powers of mesmerism, and innocent young girls about to be menaced by either or both, entirely in non-realistic settings. But at a later stage rationalism prevailed, and the main story was placed in a more realistic framework, so that the expressionistic sets of Herman Warm, Walter Röhrig and Walter Reimann became the mad narrator's vision of the world. Here the somnambulist (Conrad Veidt) makes off with the heroine (Lil Dagover) across the crazy rooftops.

▷ KING KONG (1933)
Dir. Merian C. Cooper, Ernest B. Schoedsack

Just before Beauty manages to kill the Beast (it is Kong's love for Faye Wray which precipitates disaster), King Kong, brought to New York from his remote island home, escapes from the theatre where he is being exhibited and heads inevitably for the highest building in sight. Not, evidently, the Empire State, as is usually supposed, but some futuristic fiction atop which he can swat the attacking biplanes like so many irritating mosquitoes. Kong's notional size fluctuates wildly from sequence to sequence, but the magic remains unimpaired. *Photograph by Bob Coburn*

▽ FREAKS (1932)
Dir. Tod Browning

Something not quite explained but clearly very nasty has happened to Olga Baclanova in the final sequence of *Freaks*: after the circus freaks themselves are done with her she has been transformed from the local siren trapeze artiste into some kind of a monster, half woman, half chicken. Tod Browning's horror story was otherwise notable primarily for its use of real circus freaks to play the Bearded Lady, the Elastic Man, the pin-headed twins and other weird inhabitants of the side-show half-world.

△
◁ **THE SHINING** (1980)

Dir. Stanley Kubrick

In Kubrick's almost unbearably intense
horror film, the principal character is really
the out-of-season hotel, way up in the
mountains, which exerts an evil influence
on the family looking after it for the winter.
Prime among those to be affected is the
mild-mannered Jack Nicholson, who is
gradually worked up into a murderous
frenzy against his wife (Shelley Duvall) all
the more terrifying for never being ade-
quately explained. Is the hotel again going
to manage to eat its inhabitants alive?
Ah, that, up to the very last moment, would
be telling.

▽ THE BIRDS (1963)
Dir. Alfred Hitchcock

'The Birds is coming, the Birds is coming,' cried the billboards as the première of Hitchcock's extravagant excursion into ecological nightmare approached. And come it/they did, with a vengeance. They started off in a small way by getting into Tippi Hedren's as a rule immaculately groomed hair, then stepped up their attack until by the end of the film she is in a state of catatonic shock – which says little for the humans' chances of escaping into a better, bird-free San Francisco. Today Tippi Hedren, tomorrow the world. Hedren, a personal discovery of Hitchcock's, was to receive the brunt of an extraordinary amount of his alleged misogyny in the two films she made for him.

▷ THE NIGHT OF THE HUNTER (1955)
Dir. Charles Laughton

Laughton's solitary foray into film direction created out of Davis Grubb's book a magical world where rather prosaic characters (the itinerant preacher who murders widows for their money, the woman farmer who cherishes nature and young things) become the matter of myth. A film of exquisite, highly formalized images, it gave Robert Mitchum one of his best roles as the plausible preacher, with 'love' tattooed on one hand and 'hate' on the other; it featured Shelley Winters as his pathetic victim (last glimpsed in her watery grave with her hair streaming out behind her); and sent Winters's menaced children off down the river of life into the reassuring arms of Lillian Gish.

NOSFERATU – EINE SYMPHONIE DES GRAUENS (1921)
Dir. F.W. Murnau

For obscure reasons of copyright, Murnau's classic silent version of *Dracula* had to be called something else, though since the script was considerably more faithful to Bram Stoker's book than any film actually using the name of Dracula the deception was purely formal. The vampire count of Max Schreck was, even at his most nocturnal-normal, a far more frightening creature than Bela Lugosi's (page 56), who was content to be suave and faintly sinister. Anyone observing 'Count Orlock's' arrival at Whitby could reasonably be convinced he was up to no good.

ROMANCE

LOVE WITH THE PROPER STRANGER

◁ A MAN AND A WOMAN/Un Homme et une Femme (1966)
Dir. Claude Lelouch

Jean-Louis Trintignant and Anouk Aimée, to be precise. Widowed both, they meet and love and frolic with their children in glamorous colour, swooning camera movements and more soft focus and slow motion than you could shake a filter at. The ultimate piece of romantic escape from the swing of the sixties, it stayed so potent in the public memory that twenty years on writer-director Claude Lelouch arranged a return match for his stars, called, reasonably enough, *A Man and a Woman: Twenty Years Later.*

◁ BRIEF ENCOUNTER (1945)
Dir. David Lean

The masterpiece of stiff-upper-lip English romance, *Brief Encounter* was based on a one-act play by Noël Coward, and featured Celia Johnson and Trevor Howard as the ordinary, happily married (not to each other, of course) middle-class people who find moments of stolen bliss and inescapable guilt over the Boots library books and tea and rock-cakes in the station buffet. The stars managed to express a world of emotions behind the staid inarticulate formulations, thanks to David Lean's eloquent, moody direction and to Rachmaninov's Second Piano Concerto thundering away on the sound-track.

△ CASABLANCA (1942)
Dir. Michael Curtiz

You must remember this. . . . There has proved to be an amazing number of things to remember about what began as a reasonably run-of-the-mill programmer back in 1942. It is hard to say exactly what turned an ordinary war-time romance into a myth: the extraordinary constellation of stars, the sparky romantic teaming of Humphrey Bogart and Ingrid Bergman, the song, perhaps the vividness of the relationships given that no one, not even the stars, knew which man Bergman would go off with until the end of shooting. Certainly this last gave the farewell scene its unforgettable intensity.

A PLACE IN THE SUN (1951) ▷▷
Dir. George Stevens

The question always asked about adaptations of Theodore Dreiser's novel *An American Tragedy* was, 'Is Clyde found guilty or not guilty?' The working-class hero wants to kill his tiresomely pregnant working-class girlfriend, and almost does it, though she dies accidentally and he is accused of her murder. But his real crime may be that he tries to jump out of his class and marry the rich girl instead. An easy enough crime to commit if, as in George Stevens's high-gloss version, you are Montgomery Clift and the rich girl is Elizabeth Taylor, never more beautiful and coming on strong.

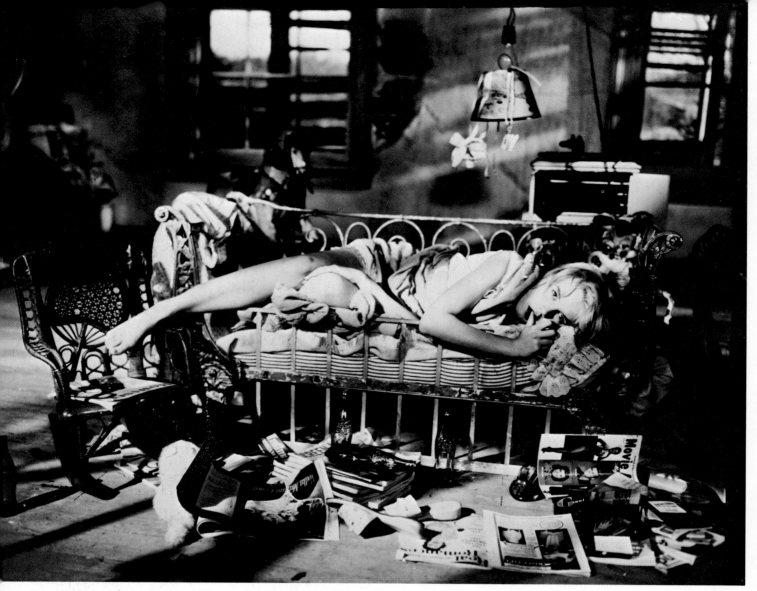

△
BABY DOLL (1956)
Dir. Elia Kazan

But of course: Carroll Baker lying in the cot she has long grown out of, sucking her thumb. It is the embodiment of Tennessee Williams's torrid comedy of the Deep South, full of Lolita-like overtones as the apparently innocent wanton sets all the local men aflame. Arguably Elia Kazan's best film, *Baby Doll* creates a powerful atmosphere compounded by Boris Kaufman's moody black-and-white photography, Richard Sylbert's suitably sleazy design, and Kenyon Hopkins's sultry score – all in support of the sexiest thumb-sucker in the business.

▷
LOLITA (1961)
Dir. Stanley Kubrick

The real thing: accept no substitutes. Critics complained that fifteen-year-old Sue Lyon was too old to play Nabokov's famous jail-bait, who is thirteen at the beginning of the story and eighteen at the end. But if they thought she was too mature, one wonders how many thirteen-year-old girls they had examined closely of late. Wearing sunglasses and licking a lollipop Lolita reduces the hapless Humbert Humbert (James Mason, brilliant as ever) to a quivering jelly; and it is all there in a single, ineradicable image, standing as well as anything but Kubrick's whole film can for his nightmare of juvenile temptation and late-flowering lust. *Photograph by Bert Stern*

▽

DEATH IN VENICE/Morte a Venezia
(1971)

Dir. Luchino Visconti

Thomas Mann in his novella managed to retain a telling ambiguity between a platonic ideal of beauty and a very corporeal boy when depicting Tadzio, the young and unapproachable lad who drives the ageing writer–hero half-mad with memory and desire in a cholera-quarantined Venice. Visconti for his film version concentrated more on the décor than the characters, though Dirk Bogarde gave a remarkable performance as the writer, half Mahler, half Mann himself. As Tadzio, Björn Andresen left nothing to be desired except that impalpability which a novelist can confer but remains forever outside a film-maker's reach.

▽

THE BLUE ANGEL/Der blaue Engel (1930)
Dir. Josef von Sternberg

Men gather to her like moths around a flame, and if their wings burn she's surely not to blame. Or maybe just a little bit, for Lola Lola was quite knowingly *fatale*, leading the silly old professor on to his ruin. At this time Marlene Dietrich, still in Germany after starring in several silent films she now denies existed, had some obvious rough edges soon to be smoothed away by Josef von Sternberg's caressing camera and the full Hollywood treatment. But the allure was unmistakable, and Emil Jannings was not the only one who fell for her husky renditions of Friedrich Hollaender's songs.

◁ ROOM AT THE TOP (1958)

Dir. Jack Clayton

In the fifties (and perhaps still) it was automatically assumed in films that English women were cold, passionless creatures, but French women – well, that was something else again. And so it was almost inevitable that while Joe Lampton, the hero of John Braine's bestselling novel, will use a rich local virgin on his way upwards and out of his Northern slum, he will get his lessons in sensuality from an older, married, French woman. And who better than Simone Signoret to teach Laurence Harvey about love? *Photograph by Eric Gray*

▽

FROM HERE TO ETERNITY (1953)

Dir. Fred Zinneman

Though by modern standards Deborah Kerr's romp in the Hawaiian surf with Burt Lancaster was pretty chaste, it rang bells at the box office partly because of who was romping (could this be the same Deborah Kerr we knew as a pure English rose in *The Prisoner of Zenda, Quo Vadis* and such?), and partly because, far from being a sensational excrescence, it was a pivotal point in the plot, bringing the colonel's lady to a showdown and a bout of bitter self-revelation with the bluff, only apparently uncomplicated Sergeant, who represents the positive side of army life. *Photograph by Irving Lippman*

85

▽ LE JOUR SE LÈVE (1939)
Dir. Marcel Carné

The climax of a series of romantic and fatalistic dramas written by Jacques Prévert and directed by Marcel Carné in the thirties, *Le Jour se Lève* had it all: the trapped gunman (Jean Gabin) waiting out the long night in a garret, helped by a few stolen moments of love with Arletty, before in the morning he goes out to certain death on the streets. Trauner's meticulously detailed yet faintly unreal sets created the atmosphere to perfection, and Gabin smoked a last cigarette and regarded the world through hooded, weary eyes the way no one else ever did.

▷
QUEEN CHRISTINA (1933)
Dir. Rouben Mamoulian

Perhaps the happiest piece of casting in Garbo's talkie career, *Queen Christina* was marred by stilted scripting and some rather lack-lustre performances in support – probably not helped by the mid-stream substitution of Garbo's erstwhile silent co-star John Gilbert for the young Laurence Olivier as the solitary queen's main romantic interest. All the same, Garbo looked handsome in what is mainly a breeches role, and the most memorable moments came in the first love scene, in which Garbo ate grapes meltingly in the flickering fire-light, and in the bleak finale which sends her off into exile with a Mona Lisa look on her face: Garbo, when asked, said firmly 'I was thinking of nothing.'

△

MAGNIFICENT OBSESSION (1954)
Dir. Douglas Sirk

Belated German *émigré* Douglas Sirk did a
bit of everything in Hollywood before
making his particular name as a specialist
in overheated emotional melodrama. The
film which primarily created that repu-
tation was *Magnificent Obsession*, the
second film version of Lloyd C. Douglas's
tear-sodden bestseller about a playboy
restored to responsibility and his interrupted medical studies by the love of a
good, blind woman (she is the widow of a
man whose life has, in effect, been sacri-
ficed for his). Inevitably he ends by saving
her sight and her life, but not before every
last drop of fake emotion has been
squeezed out of the situation. Rock Hudson
and Jane Wyman emoted valiantly.

△
KINGS ROW (1941)
Dir. Sam Wood

The high point of Ronald Reagan's acting
career (before he dwindled into a mere
President), Sam Wood's well-upholstered
small-town melodrama *Kings Row* still
offered him a relatively minor role, though
juicy. One of the town's doctors, Charles
Coburn, is a sadist with a weakness for per-
forming operations without anaesthetics,
and in this scene Reagan, tended by Ann
Sheridan as the town's leading girl from the
wrong side of the tracks, is just realizing
that, as a result of the good doctor's minis-
trations, he is now minus both legs. All
threads in the rich tapestry of small-town
American life, no doubt. *Photograph by
Madison Lacy*

◁ **THE AFRICAN QUEEN** (1951)
Dir. John Huston

The 'queen' in question is the rusty old river-boat in which heavy-drinking captain Humphrey Bogart and spinster missionary Katharine Hepburn try to escape, but instead find themselves forced to fight their own bit of Central African war against the Germans. (The date is 1914.) Inevitably, from barbed beginnings the unwillingly yoked couple finds adventure, comradeship and then love. At least, it seemed inevitable when Bogart and Hepburn did it, lashed on through the leech-infested swamps by John Huston. *Photograph by Arthur Lemon*

△ **A STAR IS BORN** (1954)
Dir. George Cukor

Second time around (or third, if you count *What Price Hollywood?*, 1932), this story of rags to riches and (simultaneously) vice versa becomes an ordeal of rather insecurely pitched emotional intensity, as obscure nightclub singer Esther Blodgett (Judy Garland) turns into a musical superstar while her alcoholic discoverer, mentor and eventually husband, roistering has-been Norman Maine (James Mason), sinks ever deeper into drink and degradation. The crunch comes when he, interrupting her acceptance of the Oscar with a drunken plea for work, inadvertently slaps her and turns the whole world against him. Garland even more jumpy than usual; Mason wonderful.

TO HAVE AND HAVE NOT (1944)
Dir. Howard Hawks

Bacall's in town and Bogart's got her. This is her début, after discovery by director Howard Hawks, and the beginning of one of Hollywood's most enduring private-life romances. Bacall, sporting what was hopefully dubbed the 'wolverine look', managed to make even a simple request for a match sound like an erotic challenge, and a little later in the involuted plot (scarcely anything to do with Hemingway's novel of the same name) delivered her famous order to Bogart, 'Just whistle. You know how to whistle, don't you Steve?' In the film, as in life, he inexorably rose to the bait. *Photograph by Mac Julian*

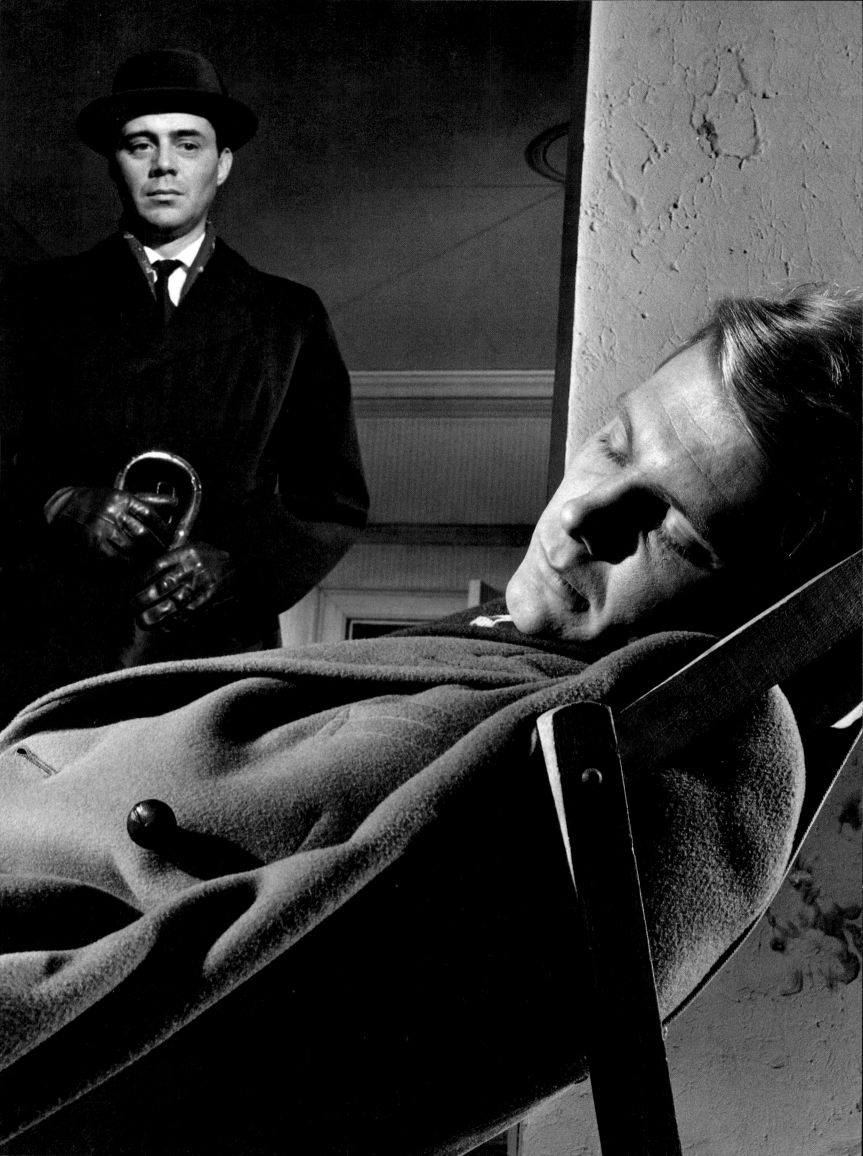

SOCIAL DRAMA

IMITATION OF LIFE

◁ **THE SERVANT** (1963)
Dir. Joseph Losey

Adapting a novella by Robin Maugham, Harold Pinter brought the true tremor of his glacial, haunted world vividly to the screen in his first collaboration with director Joseph Losey. The story turns on the precariously balanced relationship between rich idler James Fox and his sinisterly cool, obsequious manservant (Dirk Bogarde), who very soon takes control of the situation. Here the impeccably formal servant arrives in the house of his new master – very much as Mephistopheles might arrive in the house of Faust. *Photograph by Norman Hargood*

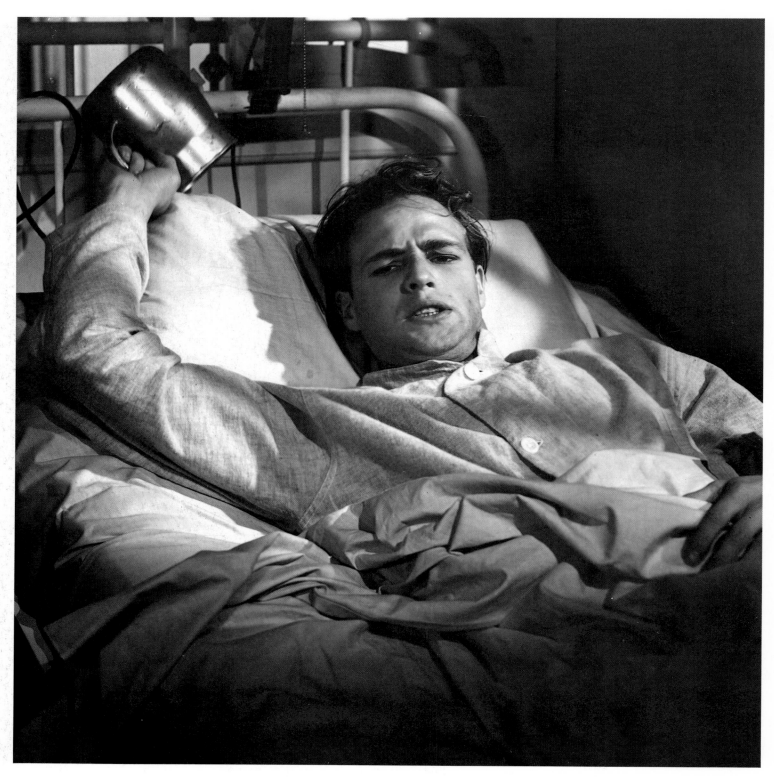

△
THE MEN (1950)
Dir. Fred Zinneman

Marlon Brando's début film would be memorable for that if nothing else. In fact it was Brando's second film, *A Streetcar Named Desire* (1951), which did much more to establish the long-lived stereotype of Brando as the uncouth Method mumbler, but even in *The Men* his powerful physicality dominates the screen, although he plays a paraplegic from World War II who fights against and finally learns to accept his lot as a permanent cripple. Otherwise the film suffers from a too-formulaic script, but benefits from the quiet, sensitive direction of Fred Zinneman.

△

EAST OF EDEN (1954)
Dir. Elia Kazan

Even thirty years after, it is possible to see at once exactly why James Dean in his brief life (only three starring films) electrified the screen and movie-goers around the world. The title of his second film, *Rebel Without a Cause* (1955), summed most of it up: the quintessence of the disaffected teenager, disdainful of his elders yet desperate for their love and acceptance, he combined strength and vulnerability with a powerful physical allure. In his début film, cunningly directed by Elia Kazan, these characteristics were even more in evidence. Most memorable scenes: the walk with his long-estranged mother, and the climax in which his stuffed-shirt father (Raymond Massey) rejects on lofty moral grounds the money he has made to retrieve the family fortunes.

△

◁ SUNSET BOULEVARD (1950)
Dir. Billy Wilder

THE DISCREET CHARM OF THE
BOURGEOISIE/Le Charme Discret de la
Bourgeoisie (1972)
Dir. Luis Buñuel

A CLOCKWORK ORANGE (1971) ▷▷
Dir. Stanley Kubrick

'All right, Mr DeMille, I'm ready for my close-up,' murmurs Norma Desmond, demented silent movie queen, as she glides down the staircase of her mouldering Hollywood mansion, out of the world inhabited by the rest of the cast and into her own happy illusion. She is playing Salome; Gloria Swanson, a far-from-demented silent survivor, is playing her – and in the performance of her lifetime, one so lifelike that many chose to believe she was merely playing herself. No chance: unlike Norma, Gloria continued to act in a real Hollywood for another thirty years or so, though this was undoubtedly her apogee.

Once a surrealist, always a surrealist, and certainly right to the end of his life Buñuel's films, even the most apparently prosaic of them, were impregnated with the spirit of surrealism. *The Discreet Charm of the Bourgeoisie* was the one in which it came closest to the surface: six friends keep trying to have dinner together, but one thing and another constantly interrupts them before they can get to the food. This time, just as they are sitting down to dine, a curtain goes up and they find that they are on stage, watched by an appreciative but critical audience which requires that they perform when they have, inconsiderately, not been provided with a script.

Kubrick's film of Anthony Burgess's futuristic novel was sinisterly accurate in its prediction of a technological society at its wits' end, beset by random violence and almost submerged in its own non-biodegradable waste. So much so that Kubrick is said now to have qualms about its being shown, in a world of mouldering tower-blocks and meaningless terrorism. Certainly the gang of 'droogs' on the rampage, led by the ebullient Malcolm McDowell, are all too recognizable today, and the film's ambiguous response to the central character (is he or isn't he the hero we identify with?) makes the film even more uncomfortable in the late eighties.

◁ PANDORA'S BOX/Die Büchse der Pandora (1928)
Dir. G.W. Pabst

Frank Wedekind's two turn-of-the-century plays about Lulu present her as 'the personification of primitive sexuality who inspires evil unaware'; G.W. Pabst in his silent film version went one step further, by making her 'sweetly innocent' as she threads her way through a world of corruption and perversity to her inevitable end at the hands of a Jack-the-Ripper-like killer. In this he was aided by the magnetic, elusive presence of Hollywood renegade Louise Brooks, whose troubling gaze can be appreciated here while, at her own wedding reception, she dances calmly with a lesbian admirer while her husband politely waits his turn for her attention.

△
L'ÂGE D'OR (1930)
Dir. Luis Buñuel

There are, actually, two unforgettable images from this Dali/Buñuel (mostly Buñuel) collaboration, the most successful of all surrealist films. The first is one most people would rather not remember: the opening shot in which what appears to be a human eye (actually a pig's) is neatly bisected by a cut-throat razor. (This is intended, in the approved surrealist fashion, to shock us into a state of free association.) The other is this, where Lya Lys, at the end of a long scene of what should be total erotic abandon were it not constantly, frustratingly, interrupted, vents her pent-up emotion on a nearby statue: one of the cinema's great sensuous images.

△

MR SMITH GOES TO WASHINGTON
(1939)
Dir. Frank Capra

After Mr Deeds had gone profitably to Town in Frank Capra's big hit of 1936, Capra tried to repeat the formula (and indeed succeeded) three years later with James Stewart replacing Gary Cooper as the innocent backwoodsman whose strength is as the strength of ten because his heart is pure. Political simpleton Stewart is put into the Senate by corrupt interests (headed by Claude Rains) because they think he will bumble their dubious schemes through without realizing what he is doing. Of course he wises up in time to engage in a giant filibuster while evidence is gathering, and even though he has a nasty shock when the evidence too proves to be rigged (here), at least truth and honour triumph in the end. *Photograph by Irving Lippman*

△

LA RÈGLE DU JEU (1939)
Dir. Jean Renoir

Revered perhaps more for what it attempted than what it achieved (not to mention its long odyssey of cutting, banning, restoration and rediscovery), Renoir's anarchic farce all takes place during a weekend house-party where the grand personages present begin with the intention of shooting a little game and end, with the enthusiastic assistance of the servants, shooting one another. Renoir based his script (remotely) on Musset's *Les Caprices de Marianne*, and himself played one of the leading roles. To begin with, things go on much as usual below stairs, despite some disturbing observations from the gamekeeper (Gaston Modot).

◁ **WAY DOWN EAST** (1920)
Dir. D. W. Griffith

Everyone remembers that in *Way Down East* Lillian Gish has to be saved from an ice-flow, but many fewer remember how and why she got there. D. W. Griffith's independent production took a creaking stage melodrama about a country girl seduced by a city slicker, turned out into the blizzard by her merciless father and saved by the simple lad from the neighbouring farm — who truly loves her — and by dint of shooting it all on actual locations brought new life to it all. The ice was as real as it looks, and that is the real Lillian Gish on it — though the real Griffith was back in New York when the sequence was filmed, recovering from injuries sustained earlier in the shooting.

△
THE KILLING FIELDS (1983)
Dir. Roland Joffe

Improbably British-made, Roland Joffe's sentimental reflections on America's involvement in Cambodia and the morality of the press in war-time was far stronger on images than argument. But the performance of real-life sufferer from the Khmer Rouge Haing S Ngov as Dith Pran, Cambodian stringer for a *New York Times* reporter and equally a character drawn from life, really tugged at the world's heartstrings. His apocalyptic progression through a Valley of Death after escaping his captors gave the cinema of the eighties some of its most potent images.

△
THE LOST WEEKEND (1945)
Dir. Billy Wilder

▷
DAYS OF WINE AND ROSES (1962)
Dir. Blake Edwards

Though it tends to look a little stilted and unconvincing now, in its day *The Lost Weekend* was quite bold for its relatively uncompromising treatment of alcoholism on screen. Wilder was also bold to cast as his tortured alcoholic Ray Milland, up to then known almost entirely as a light comedian. As with Doctor Johnson's female preacher, it was not so much that he did it well as that he did it at all; anyway he got his Oscar for a brave attempt. Here he is about to take another step on the downward track, watched by his friendly neighbourhood bartender (Howard Da Silva).

The normal assumption of exemplary tales about alcoholism is that all can be saved by the love of a good woman. Not so this time round; on the contrary, once over-social drinker Jack Lemmon has overcome the distaste of his wife Lee Remick with chocolate-flavoured cocktails, it is *folie à deux*. As things go from bad to worse, he turns out to be in a better position to kick the habit than she: moments of clarity lead to frenzy, desperation and finally liberation. At the bottom, he smashes up the contents of the greenhouse: with roses, as with wine, you can have too much of a good thing. . . .

◁ THE TIN DRUM/Die
Blechtrommel (1979)
Dir. Volker Schlöndorff

The boy plays his drum, and the world unwillingly listens. Schlöndorff's adaptation of Gunter Grass's chilling novel featured an extraordinary performance by young David Ben-nent, the twelve-year-old child of an actor, whose physical growth had, like his character's, been retarded relative to his intellectual development; and helped to break down the national barriers of cinema in Europe, reaching by the intensity of its vision a vast public which had never before con-sidered going to see a German film – and in German. Which was just as well, since at a budget of a projected 6–7 million Deutschmarks it was the most expensive film made in Germany since the war, a project a French producer described as 'artistic masochism'.

△
GREAT EXPECTATIONS
(1946)
Dir. David Lean

The earlier, and better, of Lean's two Dickens adaptations, *Great Expectations* was littered with fine performances, and incidentally introduced Alec Guinness to the cinema in the classic introductory role of hero's best friend. The dark world of Victorian London is vividly conjured up, and matched by the equally sinister country house in which the obsessed Miss Havisham lives, goading on her beautiful young ward to be her revenge on men. The moment everyone remembers, with a gasp, is near the beginning, when young Pip (Anthony Wager), before he has expectations of any kind, is grabbed by an escaped convict (Finlay Curry) in the wind-blown churchyard near his home in the bleak Thames estuary. *Photograph by Cyril Stanborough*

▽

BITTER RICE/Riso Amaro (1949)
Dir. Giuseppe De Santis

Outside Italy (and inside it, for that matter) the post-war neo-realism of Rossellini, de Sica and others was strictly highbrow, art-house stuff. But there was another brand, which used the real locations very much as Hollywood did when making films on the street 'where it really happened' became fashionable: as a vivid and (hopefully) validating background to the same old melodramatic nonsense. Guiseppe De Santis's *Bitter Rice* was interested less in the plight of downtrodden workers in the Italian rice fields than in the spectacle of Silvana Mangano, calf-high amid the alien rice, throwing out her challenge to the British Board of Film Censors.

▽

THE GRADUATE (1967)
Dir. Mike Nichols

In Charles Webb's novel and Mike Nichols's film the young hero (Dustin Hoffman) certainly had *le diable au corps* and it did not take much in the wife of one of his father's friends (Anne Bancroft), except a certain skill in organization and a great pair of legs, to bring it out. Unfortunately, once experience has shown him the way he wants to pursue it with innocence, in the shape of the obliging lady's daughter — unfortunately, that is, for the film, since with a loud grinding of gears what has been an engagingly ruthless sex comedy becomes an overwrought melodrama with Anne Bancroft as a Medea of the well-heeled surburbs.

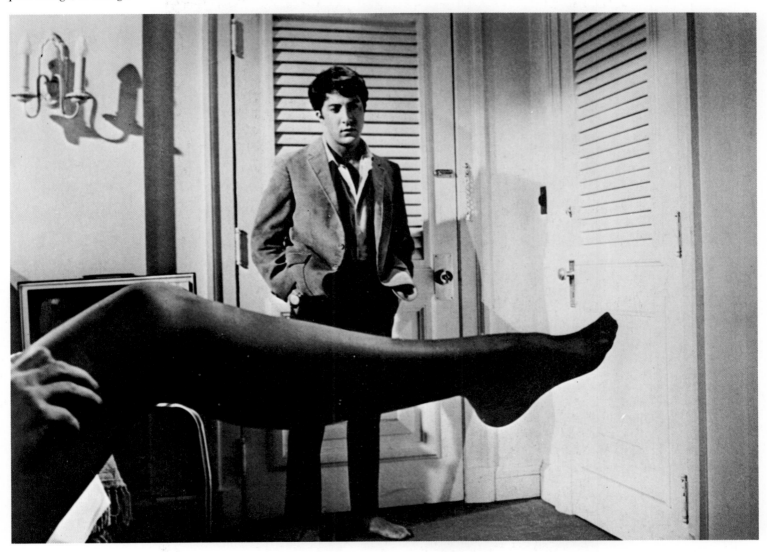

△

MIDNIGHT EXPRESS (1978)
Dir. Alan Parker

Alan Parker's raucous adaptation of Billy Hayes's quite dignified autobiographical book about his experiences in a Turkish prison after being busted for drug-smuggling imported many sensational highlights: the scene in which Billy (Brad Davis) bites off the tongue of an amorous Turkish head warder; that in which, after a highly-charged shower scene, he rejects the advances of a handsome Swedish fellow-prisoner (something he certainly did not do in the book); and the scene illustrated here, when his girlfriend (Irene Miracle) finally gets to visit him. Understandably, the Turks objected to the film, while the real Billy Hayes did a round of the TV talk-shows.

▷

LE DIABLE AU CORPS (1947)
Dir. Claude Autant-Lara

Raymond Radiguet was still a teenager himself when he wrote his definitive novel of teenage love, *Le Diable au Corps*. Gérard Philipe was twenty-five when he played the role of the schoolboy in love with an older woman, but under Claude Autant-Lara's direction he found just the mixture of vulnerability and self-absorption which anyone who has ever been a schoolboy will instantly recognize. The older woman was sensitively played by Micheline Presle, and the film itself is a monument to a sort of clear-eyed, unsentimental French romanticism which sees the truth even while it cherishes the fantasy. *Photograph by Raymond Voinquel*

◁ LA DOLCE VITA (1960)
Dir. Federico Fellini

Another breakthrough Continental movie, *La Dolce Vita* gave the term currency in the English language and created its own (probably quite unrealistic) idea of the glamorous life lived around the Via Veneto which has somehow stuck through several generations. In fact, like all Fellini's films, it takes place in a fantasy world of his own imagination, vaguely hooked on to some kind of external reality. Where else would abandon be represented by Anita Ekberg romping in the Trevi Fountain, as a visiting star who fades from hero Marcello Mastroianni's vision in yet another hopeless dawn? *Photograph by Pierluigi*

▷

WR: MYSTERIES OF THE ORGANISM/
WR: Misterije Organizma (1971)
Dir. Dušan Makavejev

Practically everything in Makavejev's wild, way-out, madly funny excursion into polemical cinema is sent up or put down, in a gleeful parity of dis-esteem. Catholics or Communists, seekers after free feminist love or the health-giving potential of Reich's orgone box – either everyone takes offence or no one does. (Actually, a lot of people did.) The nearest the film comes to a plot is the story, interwoven with the documentary and archive material, of a Yugoslavian sexual liberationist (Milena Dravić) who here visibly expresses her commitment to the theories of Wilhelm Reich, the 'WR' of the title, before she puts them into practice and is beheaded by a Soviet ice-skater because the ecstasy she induces in him is, like the film, just too much.

◁ **A MATTER OF LIFE AND DEATH** (1946)
Dir. Michael Powell, Emeric Pressburger

▽
IF... (1968)
Dir. Lindsay Anderson

CITIZEN KANE (1941) ▷▷
Dir. Orson Welles

'One is so starved for colour up there,' observes the celestial messenger who comes down the giant 'stairway to heaven' (the film's American title) from a monochrome heaven to a saturated-Technicolor earth, to take back badly injured airman David Niven for the trial which will decide whether he lives or dies. Here, before the heavenly tribunal, English doctor Roger Livesey (who is operating on him) matches the pleas of Raymond Massey, American zealot from the War of Independence, on the grounds that the love of a good American girl should redeem any errant Brit. Twaddle, transformed by the uninhibited vision of Michael Powell. *Photograph by Eric Gray*

Oddly, the image that is remembered above all from Lindsay Anderson's famous allegory of revolution in an English public school is not one of triumph and guns on the roof, but this, of ring-leader Malcolm McDowell's ritual humiliation at the hands of the prefects. It is, of course, a pivotal point in the plot: the incident that confirms the will to open revolt. But it also encapsulates the Englishman's dream/nightmare of boarding-school life, the horrors of *Tom Brown's Schooldays* nearly a century nearer Armageddon.

The world's most famous film, the challenge Orson Welles threw down to Hollywood complacency at the age of twenty-six and had to live with and down ever after, is full of great moments, as *Hamlet* is full of quotations. The career of a great, just-dead tycoon (not altogether unlike the very-much-alive Randolph Hearst) is illuminated in lightning flashes of brilliance, from his death murmuring 'Rosebud' as the snowstorm globe drops from his hand (page 1), through his rise, the pursuit of his political ambitions, and his rapidly deteriorating marriage (chronicled in a succession of blistering breakfast scenes), to his gloomy old age in the echoing halls of Xanadu, his private palace, while his mistress (Dorothy Comingore) plays endlessly with jigsaw puzzles. *Photograph by Alex Kahle*

COMEDY
MAKE 'EM LAUGH

◁ MODERN TIMES (1936)
Dir. Charles Chaplin

'That ballet-dancer', W. C. Fields contemptuously called Charlie Chaplin. Chaplin himself would probably not have rejected the description: by all accounts he was very aware of the mime and *commedia dell'arte* tradition from which his comedy sprang. In *Modern Times* he is still, as late as 1936, fighting a rearguard action against the talkies, pitting his still-silent tramp character against the dehumanization of the machine. After a spell on an assembly line which virtually turns him into a robot, Chaplin runs wild and does a mad little dance all over the machines. The film is often ruthless and cruel, but not as sentimental or pretentious as it sounds, and funnier than most of Chaplin's full-length features. *Photograph by Max Munn Antrey*

▽ **LE MILLION** (1931)
Dir. René Clair

▷
THE ROAD TO MOROCCO (1942)
Dir. David Butler

René Clair, having tried his strength on the talkie with *Sous les Toits de Paris* (1930), really mastered the new medium in *Le Million*: a musical fantasy about a wandering lottery ticket, lost in the pocket of a pawned coat, and the painter-owner's (René Lefèvre) pursuit of it. He gets involved along the way with an opera company in which his girlfriend (Annabella) is a dancer, and when his own words are not sufficient to make up a tiff he allows a pair of overweight opera stars to say it all for him.

The series of Road films, which took their stars successively to Singapore, Zanzibar, Morocco, Utopia, Rio, Bali and Hong Kong over twenty-two years, started more or less by accident when three big stars under contract to Paramount – Bing Crosby, Bob Hope and Dorothy Lamour – were brought together in a somewhat surrealistic comedy adventure and found a formula that worked: romantic sparring between Crosby and Hope, and the brisk, no-nonsense presence of Lamour as the object of their ill-directed desires. The boys had to assume endless disguises to get themselves in and out of harems and cannibal cookpots, but usually it was the long-suffering Dotty who resolved the situation without ever quite, definitively, picking her man.

▽ IT HAPPENED ONE NIGHT (1934)
Dir. Frank Capra

▷
THE BRIDE CAME C.O.D. (1941)
Dir. William Keighley

Boy meets girl, boy hates girl (and vice versa), but since they are stuck with each other they somehow battle their way through to True Love at the final fade-out. Such situations were staple to the screwball comedies of Hollywood in the thirties; but this was so as much as anything because of the fantastic success of Capra's *It Happened One Night*, which won Oscars for picture, director, script and both stars, Clark Gable and Claudette Colbert. She is a runaway heiress, he a newly fired reporter in search of a story, and in this scene they compare hitch-hiking techniques. (Hers, which involves showing a lot of silk stocking to passing motorists, wins hands down.) *Photograph by Irving Lippman*

Sweets to the sweet, they say, and no doubt the same goes for prickles. Bette Davis, taking a holiday from heavy drama, has a whale of a time as a kidnapped heiress in a so-so screwball comedy. Her father has arranged for her to be kidnapped – by James Cagney, no less – rather than make an unsuitable marriage, but the plane that is taking her homewards makes a forced landing in Death Valley, leaving the two stars to battle it out with only the cactus for company. *Photograph by Bert Six*

◁

A NIGHT AT THE OPERA
(1935)
Dir. Sam Wood

Most of the Marx Brothers' early films were based on tried and true stage successes. For the later ones, to fine-tune their comic effects, they would take a roughly assembled version of the script out on the road for a few weeks. The famous stateroom sequence in *A Night at the Opera* must have benefited from this sort of try-out: as person after person, each with his or her own single-minded pre-occupation, crowds into the shoe-box-sized stateroom, the fun gets more and more complex and contained. All that is missing to make the party complete is the statuesque Margaret Dumont, but in her absence Groucho seems to be doing all right with the manicurist.

▽

KIND HEARTS AND CORONETS (1949)
Dir. Robert Hamer

Counter-jumping Louis Mazzini, black sheep of the proud d'Ascoynes, has just disposed of two relatives standing between him and a dukedom, but there are still six to go – all played by Alec Guinness and all, by a little flourish of the special effects department, gathered together in one shot for our delight and wonderment. Robert Hamer's comedy of murders is surely the most elegant film in the whole of British cinema, and when you remember that as well as eight Guinnesses we have Dennis Price at his most stylish, Valerie Hobson at her most grandly gracious, and Joan Greenwood for all-round enchantment, it is difficult to imagine what more anyone could ask. *Photograph by Bob Penn*

△

MOVE OVER DARLING (1963)
Dir. Michael Gordon

The quip in Hollywood was that they knew Doris Day before she was a virgin. But the perpetual virgin, constantly being saved at the last from seduction even when well into her forties, took it all in good part, as she did the innumerable other indignities meted out to her in the course of her twenty-year screen career as singer, comic, romantic and occasionally dramatic figure, teamed with every leading man from Cary Grant to Rock Hudson. *Move Over Darling*, completed where angels fear to tread from the ineffable Marilyn's abortive *Something's Got to Give*, saw her teamed with James Garner and (literally) put through the wringer, trying to hide in an automatic carwash in a convertible whose hood resolutely refuses to behave as expected.

△

THE GENERAL (1926)
Dir. Buster Keaton, Clyde Bruckman

Buster Keaton has been called 'the great stone face', and also, by more fanciful French critics, 'the most beautiful animal in the world'. Both descriptions are true enough to be going on with: his famous deadpan expression carried him hilariously through stunts and adventures which would have broken up any lesser man, and the perfect grace and precision with which he carried out the most complicated and dangerous pieces of comic business often seemed almost superhuman. Here, in *The General* (which is the engine he drives at the time of the American Civil War), he tangles fearlessly with a cannon whose workings he does not begin to understand. But the Force is with him, protecting all who are truly pure at heart, and by the final fade-out he has fired the cannon, saved the train and won the girl.

◁ THE KNACK . . . AND HOW
TO GET IT (1965)
Dir. Richard Lester

Lester's iconoclastic comedy, based on a play by Ann Jellicoe, surprised everybody by winning the *Grand Prix* at the 1965 Cannes Festival and giving the whole notion of Swinging London a sparkling send-off. Rita Tushingham was almost the quintessential Swinging Sixties star – odd-looking, the ugly duckling that was clearly never going to become a swan, but funny and quirky and sexy, at any rate to those men who vie for her favours and suffer her (unjustified) accusations of rape when, a stranger in town, she finds herself sharing their bachelor pad. *Photograph by David James*

△

MONTY PYTHON'S LIFE OF
BRIAN (1979)
Dir. Terry Jones

Moving onward and (possibly) upward from their zany television series, the Monty Python team tackled the corpus of Arthurian romance in *Monty Python and the Holy Grail*, then headed fearlessly into such no-go areas for comedy as the life of Christ – or in this case Brian, any resemblance purely coincidental. They may have learnt from Mel Brooks the useful lesson, if you're going to indulge in bad taste, make it really the worst. Typical of their skilled playing on the tricky borderline between the blasphemous and the good-for-a-giggle is Brian's crucifixion, musically comforted by the good thief with 'Always Look on the Bright Side'.

▽ **THE AWFUL TRUTH** (1937)
Dir. Leo McCarey

The awful truth of the title is probably that if newly divorced Irene Dunne and Cary Grant hate each other it is because they still love eath other underneath it all. The aim of Leo McCarey's classic screwball comedy is to keep them seeing each other and out of bed with anyone else until they see this too. Very effectively managed, with a lot of inventive gags and the speed of the plot constantly deceiving the mind. Dunne is always manoeuvring with manic ingenuity, but sometimes the dog over whose custody they are squabbling gets in the way, or is over-helpful, as when he makes the concealment of a strange hat almost impossible. *Photograph by Bert Anderson*

▷
ADAM'S RIB (1949)
Dir. George Cukor

One of Hollywood's most enduring (and endearing) running battles of the sexes was that engaged in on-screen by Spencer Tracy and Katharine Hepburn, teamed first in *Woman of the Year* (1942) and finally in his last film, *Guess Who's Coming to Dinner*, twenty-five years and seven movies later. Not all their enounters were comical, but in those that were, he was generally the pillar of no-nonsense male chauvinism and she the woman who could outface any man on his own terms as well as using feminine wiles when it suited her purpose. In *Adam's Rib*, in which they are married lawyers on opposite sides in a courtroom battle, she even resorts, when cornered, to tears.

▽

EVERYTHING YOU ALWAYS WANTED TO KNOW ABOUT SEX BUT WERE AFRAID TO ASK (1972)
Dir. Woody Allen

Woody Allen's episodic sketch-film parodies Antonioni's alienated lovers, has fun with the plight of sperm waiting for blast-off, and takes side-swipes at a number of other sacred cows connected with sex. Not to mention sacred sheep, as worshipped by animal-lover Gene Wilder in one of the film's most memorable passages. And to think, at the point illustrated, the sheep, introduced into a luxury hotel room for a dirty weekend, has not yet even donned her sexy black suspender-belt.

▽

PLAY IT AGAIN, SAM (1972)
Dir. Herbert Ross

An adaptation of Woody Allen's stage play, starring him but directed by Herb Ross, *Play It Again, Sam* kept Allen's anarchic, iconoclastic humour under a tighter rein than in his own films, but was funny nevertheless as Allen's fumbling little man tries, in the aftermath of divorce, to make friends and influence people, particularly beddable girls. Which might not be too easy anyway, but is complicated by his total mental involvement in the films and roles of Humphrey Bogart, which requires him, as here, to replay scenes like the farewell from *Casablanca* (page 77), even if he does not really want to.

▷ THE SEVEN YEAR ITCH (1955)
Dir. Billy Wilder

So how could we leave out one of the most universally-known, instantly recognizable images in the whole of the twentieth century? Yet, looking at it coolly, it is difficult to explain the potency of the picture. A pretty girl showing her legs is an agreeable enough sight, but why does this particular one at this particular time so far transcend the ordinary run of cheesecake shots? The film clearly has something to do with it, as does the situation which presents Marilyn Monroe idealistically as immensely attractive and totally unaware of the effect she is having. (How would she have fared as Lulu in *Pandora's Box*, page 102, one wonders.) She is just enjoying the warmth from the subway, while Tom Ewell unaffectedly (and rather unbelievingly) enjoys her. And then, of course, it matters that this is not just any pretty girl, but M.M., already well on her way from pin-up to myth.

▽ THE SECOND HUNDRED YEARS (1927)
Dir. Fred Guiol

A fine mess you've got us into! Whether or not Ollie is saying that to the mild-eyed, melancholy Stan at this precise moment we cannot know, but he might well be. The enduring image of the Laurel-and-Hardy teaming is the Laurel and Hardy team, their mutual affection, mutual exasperation, and shared incompetence in the face of life. The trials of escaped convicts masquerading as painters may not have provided their very finest hour, but this minor disaster stands in for them all; nobody finally remains unscathed.

MUSICALS

MUSIC IN THE AIR

◁ SINGIN' IN THE RAIN (1951)

Dir. Gene Kelly, Stanley Donen

Gene Kelly, just singin', and dancin', in the rain, provides the unforgettable moment from the best darned musical Hollywood ever made. A witty spoof of Hollywood at the coming of sound, it is full of good things, great numbers and splendid performances, from Kelly as the singing swashbuckler, Donald O'Connor as his musical sidekick, Debbie Reynolds as the movie-mad singer, and Jean Hagen as the idiot movie queen ('What do you think I am – dumb or something?'). But Kelly never bettered his solitary outburst of ecstasy as the studio tanks did their worst with the studio street.

△
THE SOUND OF MUSIC (1965)
Dir. Robert Wise

▷
TOP HAT (1935)
Dir. Mark Sandrich

Though Julie Andrews was done out of her chance to play in Hollywood's *My Fair Lady* (page 151), she hit back right away with two bigger hits of her own, Walt Disney's *Mary Poppins* (1964) and *The Sound of Music*, which finally did the impossible by displacing *Gone With the Wind* (pages 178-9) from its position as number one box-office champion. Certainly her crisp and unsentimental performance as the eventual Maria von Trapp, stepmother of the Trapp Family Singers, took the curse off the rather over-saccharine stage original by Rodgers and Hammerstein, while Wise's direction kicked off in fine style with a sweeping aerial view which finally swoops down into a close shot of Julie whilst the sound-track belts out the title song.

In his autobiography, *Steps in Time*, Fred Astaire recounts how the 'Cheek to Cheek' number from *Top Hat* was one of the most troublesome he ever shot with Ginger Rogers because her blue satin dress kept shedding its feathers all over the place. Eventually they were all secured and shooting could continue on what remains one of the high points in all the Astaire–Rogers films. The song by Irving Berlin, the locale supposedly Venice, and the plot a farrago of mistaken identities which allows plenty of opportunity for girl to hate boy even though she loves him really – a situation which makes for some piquant dance duos if nothing else.

▽ SHOWBOAT (1936)
Dir. James Whale

Whatever people forget about *Showboat* on stage or screen, they always remember that Paul Robeson sang 'Ole Man River'. In the first talkie version, directed by horror-monster specialist James Whale in one of his lighter moments, Paul Robeson sang it as he had in the original British stage production and on many another occasion, to the extent that it became almost his signature. Otherwise, the film was a charming essay in nostalgia, not stinting in its depiction of the sufferings of the unfortunate Julie who tries to pass for white, but otherwise rather dated in its ethnic attitudes.

▷ THE RED SHOES (1948)
Dir. Michael Powell, Emeric Pressburger

Not exactly a musical in the ordinary sense of the term, but a film built entirely round classical ballet. When monomaniac, Diaghilev look-alike, impresario Lermontov (Anton Walbrook) asks neophyte Vickie Page 'Why do you want to dance?' she snaps back, very crisp and British, 'Why do you want to live?' As you might expect, there is a lot more than that going on in her troubled psyche, especially when it looks as though she may have to choose between dancing and true love. Most of her confusions come out in the central ballet sequence, when she rapidly leaves the stage for the astral plain and is haunted by zombies on her journey between heaven and hell. *Photograph by George F. Cannons*

△
MEET ME IN ST LOUIS (1944)
Dir. Vincente Minnelli

▷
BABES IN ARMS (1939)
Dir. Busby Berkeley

Most gentle and nostalgic of musicals, *Meet Me in St Louis* enshrined for ever a particular American view of a turn-of-the-century age of innocence (the other side of *Kings Row*, page 89) and the fresh appeal of the young Judy Garland, directed here by her husband-to-be Vincente Minnelli. Judy's big hit was 'The Trolley Song', but the best-remembered sequences are Margaret O'Brien's long Hallowe'en walk and the Christmas Eve sequence, full of yearning for things about to be lost if the family moves away from St Louis before the 1903 Exposition. Needless to say, they don't.

In the late thirties it seemed that Mickey Rooney and Judy Garland were always urging each other to put-on-a-show with the thought that 'There's this great old barn just down the road.' The great old barn generally turned out to be a well-equipped MGM sound-stage, and the numbers performed there (prior to Broadway, of course) were elaborate to the nth degree. In *Babes in Arms* the kids of old washed-up vaudevillians put on their own hit show: among the numbers is a sketch called 'The Fireside Chat', in which Judy and Mickey deliver one, and eight cuties listen in on their individual bakelite portables.

SMALL TOWN GIRL (1952) ▷▷
Dir. Leslie Kardos
THE GANG'S ALL HERE (1943)
Dir. Busby Berkeley
GOLD DIGGERS OF 1933 (1933)
Dir. Mervyn LeRoy

Busby Berkeley was a stage dance director who came to prominence in the early thirties with his fantastic, semi-abstract musical numbers, full of astonishing camera effects and chorines with chubby legs. As a rule they were spotted interchangeably into putting-on-a-show stories, with little or no relevance to the plot and indeed no conceivable possibility of being put on any stage this side of paradise (witness 'The Shadow Waltz' and the 'My Forgotten Man' finale from *Gold Diggers of 1933*, below right and left. In the forties and early fifties Berkeley usually found himself providing specialities for stars with some small, particular talent – parodying Carmen Miranda's extravagant costumes in 'The Lady in the Tutti-Frutti Hat' (*The Gang's All Here*, top right) or letting Ann Miller tap her way round a largely invisible orchestra in 'I've Gotta Hear That Beat' (*Small Town Girl*, top left).

◁ **BROADWAY MELODY OF 1940** (1940)
Dir. Norman Taurog

A putting-on-a-show story of more than usual inanity, *Broadway Melody of 1940* still goes down in the annals of unforgettable movies for two reasons. First, it introduced to the waiting movie public one of Cole Porter's best songs ever, 'Begin the Beguine', given the full treatment here in tap, swing and romantic adagio. Second, it was the only time that those two supremely disparate dance stars of the thirties, Fred Astaire and Eleanor Powell, met on screen. It might have been disaster, but rivalry brought out the best in both, and when they went into their dance they touched a height of elegance never matched before or since.

△
MY FAIR LADY (1964)
Dir. George Cukor

'Move yer arse', the lady cries, to the consternation of all at Cecil Beaton's elegant black-and-white Ascot. Of course, Shaw's original Eliza Doolittle could provoke the same effect with no more than 'Not bloody likely', but time does march on. The film of the Lerner-and-Loewe musical remained in George Cukor's hands gracefully stagy (he blamed Beaton for that), but once all the fuss had died down about Julie Andrews not getting 'her' role we could all appreciate Audrey Hepburn as a radiant ugly duckling turned swan. Even if she did need Marni Nixon to help with the singing.

151

▽
WEST SIDE STORY (1961)
Dir. Robert Wise, Jerome Robbins

The stage show conceived and choreographed by Jerome Robbins was one the the great successes of the fifties: a modern Romeo and Juliet story with script by Arthur Laurents, lyrics by Stephen Sondheim and music by Leonard Bernstein, it created a brilliant abstraction of ethnic relations between New York gangs representing native-born kids (the Jets) and immigrant Puerto Ricans (the Sharks). Originally Robbins was signed up as sole director of the film version, but then the old pro Robert Wise was brought in to snap things up a bit. The real problem remains the conversion of something designed according to stage convention into something suitable for shooting on real streets in a real city. Still, energy levels remain high when the Jets go into their dance.

▽

FLYING DOWN TO RIO (1933)
Dir. Thornton Freeland

The film that began the Fred Astaire–Ginger Rogers teaming was designed to showcase the talents of stars Dolores Del Rio and Gene Raymond, not to mention Latin charmer Raul Roulian, with the singing-and-dancing duo as picturesque support. But the paying public were in no doubt what they wanted, and the conse-quence was the deathless series of nine films in which, without doubt, Astaire and Rogers starred. None of them was terribly expensive, but *Flying Down to Rio* was the cheapest of all; but then if anything the shameless back projections against which the chubby chorines 'fly' lend a certain period enchantment to the view.

▷
NEW YORK, NEW YORK (1977)
Dir. Martin Scorsese

Scorsese's affectionate tribute to the sort of film they used to make about getting on in show business took a lot of its pictorial style from the paintings of Edward Hopper, and its climactic big number (eliminated, then restored) from the Judy Garland *A Star is Born* (1954) and/or *Inside Daisy Clover* (1966). For the rest, it depended on the barbed musical-cum-personal relationship of the two stars, jazz saxophonist Robert De Niro and singer/film star Liza Minnelli, here at its very beginning. The main difference between the film and its models was that boy got girl, boy lost girl, and she stayed lost right to the end.

△ YANKEE DOODLE DANDY (1942)
Dir. Michael Curtiz

When he was not busy on the wrong side of the law, James Cagney sometimes took time out to be a spunky all-American. And who more so than the immortal, insufferable George M. Cohan, creator of 'Yankee Doodle Dandy' and a two-hundred-per-cent patriot. Apart from anything else, the role in a biopic enabled Cagney to don his tap shoes again and remind us he started out as a hoofer, chorus-boy and occasional female impersonator. Nothing queer about our George, however, who seldom went anywhere without Uncle Sam and the Statue of Liberty in tow. *Photograph by Mac Julian*

WESTERNS

THE CODE OF THE WEST

◁ THE GREAT TRAIN ROBBERY (1903)
Dir. Edwin S. Porter

After audiences had been stampeded by the vividness of the illusion that a train was coming right at them in Lumière's *Arrival of the Paris Express* (1895), the next major ordeal they were put through was to have a gun pointed straight at them in Edwin S. Porter's *The Great Train Robbery* – and fired full in their face. This gave the film, a capsule version of a currently popular stage melodrama, its place in the history books. More than forty years later Hitchcock did the same thing in *Spellbound*, but he needed a red flash in a black-and-white film to make a comparable effect.

◁◁ THE MAGNIFICENT SEVEN (1960)
Dir. John Sturges

▽
DUEL IN THE SUN (1946)
Dir. King Vidor

▷
FOR A FEW DOLLARS MORE/Per qualche
Dollari in più (1965)
Dir. Sergio Leone

Though Sturge's Western *The Magnificent Seven* was as American as apple pie, its source was Japan, of all places, and Akira Kurosawa's immensely successful period action picture *Seven Samurai* (1954). In both films the seven wandering mercenaries are hired by a hard-pressed village to protect it from bandits. Here are the American seven, being magnificent as they ride over the hill and into action. Yul Brynner centre-screen, with Steve McQueen and Charles Bronson to extreme left and right; completing the band, James Coburn, Horst Buchholz. Brad Dexter and Robert Vaughn – but personal identity was not exactly the name of the game.

Otherwise known in Hollywood as 'Lust in the Dust', David O. Selznick's super-Western had it all: a passionate half-breed heroine (Jennifer Jones), a hero (Gregory Peck) described by the producer as 'the worst son of a bitch that's ever been seen on a motion picture screen', train-wrecking, hundreds of horsemen gathering, Tilly Losch dancing, and Lionel Barrymore in tears at the foot of the dying Lillian Gish's bed. As though that were not enough, hero and heroine have to end by shooting each other, then crawling over the rocks to die in each other's arms. King Vidor directed, with help from William Dieterle and Josef von Sternberg.

The first appearance of 'The Man With No Name' in *A Fistful of Dollars* (1964) instantly catapulted its star Clint Eastwood, its director Sergio Leone, and the whole genre it epitomized – the European-made 'Spaghetti Western' – to international fame and fortune. It instantly spawned a sequel, *For a Few Dollars More*, pictorially showy, dramatically simple, and much more bloody than any American-made Western had dared to be. The final gun battle turns on a trick with a chiming watch, in which Clint Eastwood, able to think quicker, draw faster and perhaps cheat a little into the bargain, inevitably emerges the victor.

◁ THE MAN FROM LARAMIE
(1955)

Dir. Anthony Mann

The indestructible James Stewart found a new lease of screen life in the early fifties playing attractively weathered Western heroes. Several of the best examples were directed by Anthony Mann, notably *Winchester 73*, *Bend of the River*, *The Naked Spur*, *The Far* *Country* (all 1951–5) and *The Man from Laramie*, which effectively ended the cycle. In it Stewart plays a vengeful cowman tracking down the men who killed his brother. At the time some of the trials he goes through, or puts others through, seemed surprisingly brutal for a Western, though their brutality was nothing compared with what was coming to the Western from Italy.

△
SHANE (1953)

Dir. George Stevens

Alan Ladd is a traditionally lonely gunfighter who achieves a brief respite when a decent farming family takes him in, incognito. Inevitably his past catches up with him: he has to shoot it out and move on. But not before he has played a radical role in the greening of his hosts' young son, Brandon de Wilde. The whole thing is a bit too self-consciously mythologizing for comfort, with Shane standing in for the knight errant of medieval romance, but the empty Wyoming landscapes and Shane's last ride off into the blue distance are unforgettable.

◁ **DESTRY RIDES AGAIN** (1939)
Dir. George Marshall

The original Destry may have
been one hell of a guy, but what
are we to make of his son
(James Stewart), who comes in
to clean up the town with a nice
line in cracker-barrel philoso-
phy and (apparently) no guns?
Of course, in the end he proves
more than a match for the local
villains, but meanwhile he is
called on to perform some of the
less heroic duties of a sheriff,
including breaking up a bar-
room brawl between two rival
beauties, Marlene Dietrich (of
all people, fresh from growling
'See What the Boys in the Back
Room Will Have') and Una
Merkel. *Photograph by Sher-
man Clark*

▷ **THE WILD BUNCH** (1969)
Dir. Sam Peckinpah

Peckinpah's *magnum opus*
may or may not be, as Pauline
Kael described it, 'a traumatic
poem of violence, with imagery
as ambivalent as Goya's', but it
is undeniably a memorable
piece of movie-making. Clearly
1913 was a bad time for the out-
laws of the old West: with the
traditional outlaw heroes being
reduced in the popular imagination to small-time killers, they
had little alternative but to seek
refuge in Mexico and get killed
in their turn. A simple story
made to carry a weight of
symbolic significance, *The Wild
Bunch* ends with the extinction
of the last remaining, in a wel-
ter of gory slow motion (behind
the gun, their leader William
Holden.)

◁

STAGECOACH (1939)
Dir. John Ford

The archetypal John Ford sequence: the stagecoach makes its way across Monument Valley, full of assorted heroic and comical characters, while the immemorial rock formations that Ford loved so dearly look impassively on. Of course the Indians are getting ready to attack, and of course John Wayne is on hand to protect the good and dispatch the bad. Being a relatively early Ford Western, *Stagecoach* is a black-and-white picture, in more than one sense of the term.

▽

SHE WORE A YELLOW RIBBON (1949)
Dir. John Ford

The perfect image of the cavalry Western: the stockaded fort in the middle of nowhere, with the solitary rider at the gate. The solitary rider in this case is John Wayne, a commander about to retire from a West overshadowed by Custer's defeat at Little Big Horn, and the film is less an action piece in John Ford's more familiar manner than a meditation on courage, violence, life and death, carried out against backgrounds of more than usual pictorial splendour. *Photograph by Alex Kahle*

◁◁ BUTCH CASSIDY AND THE SUNDANCE KID (1969)
Dir. George Roy Hill

The classic male-bonding Western adventure story, with the eponymous heroes incarnated by two stars of the first magnitude, Robert Redford and Paul Newman. Though their story comes over as heroic and for the most part cheerful, even comical, the undertones are all melancholy as they are hounded from place to place, forever looking over their shoulders to check the skyline and wonder 'Who are those guys?' Since it is vaguely founded on fact, it does not and it cannot come to good, but the film's makers no doubt cried all the way to the bank.

▽ GUNFIGHT AT THE O.K. CORRAL (1957)
Dir. John Sturges

And here it is: the classic encounter at dawn between the good guys and the bad guys. Only here it may be various shades of bad, depending on what you think of making such famous gun-fighters of the Old West as Wyatt Earp (played by Burt Lancaster) and Doc Holliday (Kirk Douglas) into heroes. In the course of the film Earp produces the traditional formulation: 'All gunfighters are lonely. They live alone and they die without a dime, a woman or a friend.' Here are several about to do so at the famous Corral.

▷ HIGH NOON (1952)
Dir. Fred Zinneman

Time for another showdown. The weak and timid townsfolk crowd into the church and hide from the light of day, leaving their sheriff (Gary Cooper) alone to face the gunmen who menace their peace and prosperity. Inevitably he triumphs, and leaves the town to reflect on its own spinelessness after grinding his sheriff's badge into the dust. Too self-consciously allegorical (it was, after all, made in the heyday of McCarthy), the film nevertheless offered Cooper the classic among his later roles, and introduced Grace Kelly as the sheriff's ill-used bride.

◁ LITTLE BIG MAN (1970)
Dir. Arthur Penn

Arthur Penn turns Thomas Berger's picaresque novel, a sort of American *Candide* in which the hero (Dustin Hoffman) veers wildly between red and white cultures, into a broken-backed movie in which the serious business of Custer's last stand mates uncomfortably with the eccentrically comic insights of the rest. The ending retrieves a lot, though: the hero's Indian 'grandfather' (Chief Dan George) has one of those unquestionable insights that he is about to die, goes up the mountain to do it, but then when rain stops play comes philosophically down again to live another day. *Photograph by Mel Traxel*

▽
A MAN CALLED HORSE (1970)
Dir. Elliot Silverstein

If English aristocrats are guaranteed (in movies, anyway) to be effete, there is nothing like a few years living as an American Indian to harden them up. When English milord Richard Harris is captured by the Indians in 1825 he decides to make the best of a bad job and adopt their way of life – to such effect that finally he becomes their chief. Along the way the hardening process can be pretty tough and bloodthirsty: the worst of the initiations he has to undergo is being suspended by his nipples.

ONCE UPON A TIME IN THE WEST/
C'era una Volta il West (1968)
Dir. Sergio Leone

Leone may not be much of a one for urging
the action forward – most of his 'Spaghetti
Westerns' unroll endlessly – but no one
could deny that he has an extraordinary eye
for the telling tableau. By the time he made
Once Upon a Time in the West, he was even
taking his (by now) very expensive produc-
tions on location in the real West: this film
was made partly in Utah and Arizona, as
well as in that old Spanish stand-by of
European Westerns, Almeria. In this
sequence Frank's gang (Jack Elam, Woody
Strode and Al Mulock) wait for Harmonica
(Charles Bronson) – but it might just as
well be 'The Man With No Name' himself,
Clint Eastwood, who made Leone's name
and his own in *A Fistful of Dollars*.

EPICS

THE GREATEST SHOW ON EARTH

◁ PATTON (1969)

Dir. Franklin J. Schaffner

Shaffner's spectacular biography of World War II General Patton is a portrait at once of the obsessive as hero and the hero as obsessive. Dominated (to the virtual exclusion of everyone else) by ex-marine George C. Scott's bludgeoning, unstoppable performance as Patton, man, monster and demi-god, the film manages to have its cake and eat it, making him simultaneously absurd and charismatic. Incidentally, Scott made history (of a sort) by being awarded the 1970 Best Actor Oscar and refusing it – an example followed two years later by Marlon Brando.

▷
▽ ## GONE WITH THE WIND
(1939)

Dir. Victor Fleming

If *Citizen Kane* (page 119) is not the most famous film ever made, then *Gone With the Wind* surely is. One is the supreme statement in American cinema of the film-maker as individual artist, the other is the ultimate product of the Hollywood machine. Pulp fiction elevated (almost) to high art, it chronicles the on-again, off-again, fought-against passion of Rhett Butler (Clark Gable) and Scarlett O'Hara (Vivien Leigh) against a sweeping panorama of the American Civil War, and because superb production values were matched by immaculate casting it managed to keep the two elements in perfect balance. Whether the perverse heroine was at last in the arms of the right man or picking her way through the dying and the dead in Atlanta, you always knew whom you were supposed to care about, and you did. *Photographs by Fred Parrish*

◁ CAPTAIN BLOOD (1935)
Dir. Michael Curtiz

▽ THE ADVENTURES OF ROBIN HOOD
(1938)
Dir. Michael Curtiz, William Keighley

Quite possibly Errol Flynn was not the greatest dramatic talent who ever trod the stages of Warner Brothers, but for athletic charm and derring-do there was no one to match him. In partnership, usually, with director Michael Curtiz he played in several swashbuckling classics in the thirties, starting with *Captain Blood* in 1935, climaxing in *The Adventures of Robin Hood* in 1938, and running to *The Sea Hawk* in 1940. In all of them he gets many chances to flash his smile, cross swords with assorted villains (in both these films Basil Rathbone, the best sneerer in the business), get the girl and live to fight another day. *Photographs by Mac Julian*

BEN HUR (1959) ▷▷
Dir. William Wyler

The first American *Ben Hur* (1925) was strewn with problems: at first MGM meant to shoot it all in Italy, where *Cabiria* and most good spectacles of the day came from. But then endless production difficulties forced them back to Southern California and the arena for the climactic chariot race between the noble Ben Hur and the scheming Messala was built in Culver City. In William Wyler's all-talking, all-singing, all-dancing version, the venue was shifted back to Cinecittà, with rather more satisfactory results: Charlton Heston and Stephen Boyd (not to mention sundry stunt-men) were the contestants this time round. *Photograph by Davis Boulton*

▽ GALLIPOLI (1981)
Dir. Peter Weir

▷
RAIDERS OF THE LOST ARK (1981)
Dir. Steven Spielberg

Peter Weir's answer to the sentimental atti-
tudinizing of Anthony Asquith's *Tell
England* of 1930, with its beautiful young
men going out to die nobly for their
country, was an angry diatribe against that
same England for sending hundreds of
Australians needlessly to their death in a
war which did not concern them. Still, the
young men were just as beautiful: here is
one of them (Mel Gibson) setting out on his
fruitless run to take a message through the
Turkish guns.

Here they come again, as the Thurber
characters observed of the harpies at the
dinner-table. Harrison Ford was Indiana
Jones, and boy, did he have to pay heavily
for the privilege. An unending series of
daredevil exploits and skin-of-the-teeth
escapes begins, properly enough, with pursuit by a mammoth mothball through the
treasure-stacked undercrofts of the pre-
Columbian world. And to think it could all
happen to a quiet-living (albeit husky)
archaeology professor. . . .

◁ THE PRIVATE LIFE OF HENRY VIII (1933)
Dir. Alexander Korda

Hungarian *émigré* Alexander Korda's first serious attempt to break a British film into the American market was crowned with success when Charles Laughton's rumbustious performance as the much-married monarch carried all before it and won him the year's Best Actor Oscar. The victory proved delusory, as a later succession of costly flops would testify, but the film itself, though fairly crude and cheap, is still alive and kicking. And who can forget Henry's brusque way with roast chicken, as he plonkingly proclaims 'Refinement's a thing of the past'? *Photograph by Tonbridge*

▽ THE SIGN OF THE CROSS (1932)
Dir. Cecil B. DeMille

DeMille was famed, among other things, for his fascination with baths and his determination to get as many of his heroines as possible into them. No doubt the most famous example comes in *The Sign of the Cross*, his lurid account of the arrival of Christianity at the court of Nero. The goodies around the place are as boring as goodies usually are, but the baddies, represented primarily by Charles Laughton as Nero and Claudette Colbert (of all people) as his unscrupulous empress Poppaea, are wild and wonderful, and there is no denying that Colbert looks good in hundreds of gallons of guaranteed-genuine asses' milk – even if the smell after two days of shooting was unspeakable. *Photograph by William Thomas*

▽ THE TEN COMMANDMENTS (1956)
Dir. Cecil B. DeMille

DeMille's first film called *The Ten Commandments* (1923) was one of those stories, popular at the time, which illustrate a contemporary tale with action highlights from some vaguely parallel biblical episode. The second time he parted the Red Sea it was for a full-scale re-enactment of the life of Moses, the travails of Israel in Egypt, the Dance round the Golden Calf and all that. With such unlikely ancient Egyptians as Edward G. Robinson and Anne Baxter, a lot of it was more comical than impressive. But when Charlton Heston (who else?) came down the mountain with the Tablets of the Law, at least everyone stopped and listened.

▷ THE THREE MUSKETEERS (1921)
Dir. Fred Niblo

Artless Westerner Douglas Fairbanks began in films as an unusually athletic, breezy, devil-may-care all-American boy. Before long he had risen, with his second wife Mary Pickford, to be uncrowned king of Hollywood, from which lofty position he ran his own production company, was one of the founders of United Artists (along with Mary Pickford, Charlie Chaplin and D. W. Griffith), and had launched into far more expensive costume spectacles like *Robin Hood* (1922), *The Thief of Bagdad* (1924) and *The Black Pirate* (1926). And, of course, *The Three Musketeers*, in which he could romp and duel and kid and swash-buckle to his heart's content – and, be it said, to the supreme content of his audiences too.

◁ **DIE NIBELUNGEN** (1924)
Dir. Fritz Lang

△
MOBY DICK (1956)
Dir. John Huston

Fritz Lang's giant diptych, *Siegfried* and *Kriemhild's Revenge* did for the legendary past what *Metropolis* (page 48) did for the putative future. A vast fresco, its first part, leading up to the death of Siegfried (here) at the hands of Brünnhilde, is majestically paced and rather static, while the second, in which Kriemhild (Siegfried's widow) avenges him in a bath of blood and flames, sparks with violent action. The studio-built forest was demolished by none other than Alfred Hitchcock, who needed the stage for one of the sets he had designed for *The Blackguard* (1925), shot in German studios.

'Have you read *Moby Dick*? . . . It's about this whale . . .', volunteered the intrepid cocktail party conversationalist. And so it is – the great white whale of Herman Melville's imagination. But it is also about the madness of the quest, man's endless search for the antagonist worthy of him. John Huston's film version did not come as close to this as Orson Welles's improvisatory stage version, possibly because Gregory Peck was rather wooden for the demented Captain Ahab, but the seascapes were elegantly re-created in whaling-print colours and the climactic battle between man and whale was impressively staged.

▽ **THE VICTORS** (1963)
Dir. Carl Foreman

Carl Foreman's solitary excursion as writer–producer–director, *The Victors* suffered from an excess of heavily verbalized liberal sentiment about war and some stodgy playing not helped or enlivened by the inexperienced director. But it almost pulled its chestnuts out of the fire with a stunning final sequence, in which the victims of a court martial are marched out into the snow and executed, all in long-shot, with Frank Sinatra singing 'Have Yourself a Merry Little Christmas' on the sound-track.

▷
IVAN THE TERRIBLE, PART I/Ivan Graznyi (1944)
Dir. Sergei Eisenstein

Early in his career Eisenstein cunningly dissimulated his aestheticism by dealing mainly with contemporary history, so that critics mistook him for some kind of realist. Later, the same sensibility expressed itself in more evidently hieratic (or maybe operatic) terms, in historical epics such as *Alexander Nevsky* (1938) and the two parts of *Ivan the Terrible* (with a staging of Wagner's *Siegfried* in between). Here, at the end of Part One, Ivan has gone into a voluntary retreat to recover from the murder of his beloved wife. But the people will not let him be: in their thousands they trek out to beg him to reassume control of the state.

◁ INTOLERANCE (1916)
Dir. D.W. Griffith

In 1916 indubitably the biggest, and seventy years later still the best, piece of sheer spectacle ever filmed. In those days, before the advent of armies of special effects men, if you wanted to create the impression of Babylon before its fall you had to build it all yourself, full-size, and people it with thousands of real, live extras. D.W. Griffith was already an expert at making the most of the most: with *Birth of a Nation* (1915) already under his belt, the Babylonian epic of *Intolerance*'s four stories (all dealing with Man's inhumanity to Man) was relative child's play. For years the ruins of the set were a tourist attraction just outside Los Angeles; now they are the subject of serious archaeological excavation.

▽ SPARTACUS (1960)
Dir. Stanley Kubrick

Stanley Kubrick found himself on unfamiliar territory when Anthony Mann, who had prepared this toga-clad epic, disagreed with star–producer Kirk Douglas and refused to direct it. Naturally he turned in a stylish, intelligent job, though one feels that perhaps his heart was not in it. Nevertheless, the mechanics of a gladiator's life and work has seldom been given a clearer exposition: the workings of the gladiator's school are subjected to a crisp, unromanticized once-over and the performances of a distinguished cast are well above the DeMille average for this sort of enterprise. It reminds us that a little liberal gesture like refusing to kill a gallant opponent could, even then, start a rebellion that would topple an empire.

▽ SAMSON AND DELILAH
(1949)
Dir. Cecil B. DeMille

For the scene in DeMille's epic where Samson has to demolish the temple of the Philistines single-handed – clearly the *scene à faire*, as the French say – Hedy Lamarr wore her best peacock robe and Victor Mature, his hair by this time somewhat recovered from the shearing, wore rather unfunctional chains and hessian Bermuda shorts. The stylistic antecedents of the temple were hazy too, but there were few to beat De Mille at his own game: it might be nonsense, and tacky nonsense at that, but the world was somehow persuaded to watch and remember.

▷
THE RAINS CAME (1939)
Dir. Clarence Brown

They actually came at least twice, once in black-and-white and traditional shape in the 1939 version of Louis Bromfield's novel, and once in CinemaScope and colour in the 1955 version, retitled *The Rains of Ranchipur*. On balance the spectacle of the first, with thousands of Indians swept away by the bursting dam which resolves all the characters' emotional problems at one fell swoop, was preferable to the tatty process-work of the second, itself ill-served by enlargement. The cast was better the first time too: Myrna Loy, George Brent and Tyrone Power seemed to believe it all, which is more than can be said of Lana Turner, Fred MacMurray and Richard Burton in the second.

◁ THE BRIDGE ON THE RIVER KWAI (1957)
Dir. David Lean

Though William Holden was brought into David Lean's adaptation of Pierre Boulle's novel about a Japanese prison-camp, and though his role was built up to ensure Hollywood star-power, the film was stolen by Alec Guinness as the stiff-necked English colonel, Nicholson, who persists monomaniacally along his line of action even though (as here) struck and humiliated by the Japanese commanding officer and derided by his men. In the end he wins grudging respect, even if he cannot see that the only thing to do, after building the bridge for the Japanese, is to blow it up for the Allies.

▽

JEZEBEL (1938)
Dir. William Wyler

If only Bette Davis had not been so pig-headed as to insist on wearing the flaming red dress at the débutante's ball when all the other girls were in virginal white, all might have turned out right: she could have married and been tamed by the strong but conventional Henry Fonda. Instead, what with the shame and embarrassment of it all, he goes off and marries mild-mannered Margaret Lindsay instead. But even so, Bette gets (predictably) the best of the picture, raging and suffering grandly and in the end pushing the weakling wife off-screen while she goes off to expiate all by nursing her love back to health on Plague Island. *Photograph by Schuyler Crail*

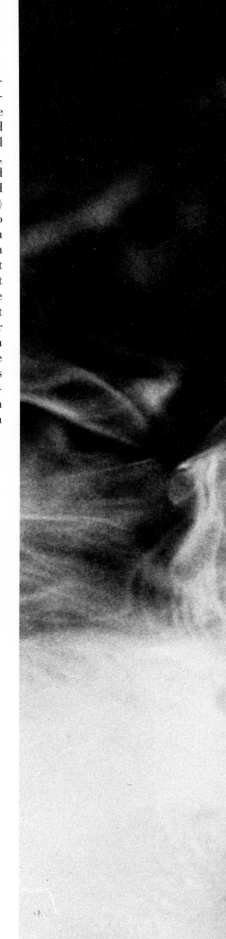

APOCALYPSE NOW (1979)
Dir. Francis Ford Coppola

Where other American film-makers, faced with the awkward fact of Vietnam, have found blood and glory or a good excuse to beat their liberal breasts at the awfulness of it all, Francis Ford Coppola turned instead to a Joseph Conrad novel (*The Heart of Darkness*) which Welles always wanted to film, and located its main action in terms of the Vietnam War. Finally the film was not really about that specific war at all, but about all war, about the collision of cultures, and about what happens to men under unbearable stress. As Martin Sheen plunges towards the heart of the darkness, he gets nearer and nearer the legendary figure that only Marlon Brando (or perhaps Welles in his heyday) was born to play.

CLEOPATRA (1963)
Dir. Joseph L. Mankiewicz

Not by any stretch of the imagination better than DeMille's *Cleopatra* of 1934 (which was no great shakes anyway), at least the Mankiewicz version was unarguably bigger. Bigger generally meant substituting sheer numbers and physical scale for an exercise of the imagination; but sometimes the millions spent on it were not enough. The casting of Elizabeth Taylor, one critic wrote, simply meant that there was a mouse at the centre of the mountain. And though her entry into Rome looks impressive in the stills, the film itself tells another story, with the skin-deep lath and plaster construction mercilessly exposed in the shadows that fall unwanted on the mobile sphinx's back.

▽ THRONE OF BLOOD/Kumonosu-Ju (1957)
Dir. Akira Kurosawa

▷

AGUIRRE, WRATH OF GOD/Aguirre,
der Zorn Gottes (1972)
Dir. Werner Herzog

As noted in connection with *The Magnificent Seven* (pages 158-60), the cultural traffic between East and West goes both ways. If Americans borrow from Kurosawa, Kurosawa equally takes his themes from Western sources, notably from Gorky for *The Lower Depths* (1957) and Shakespeare for *Throne of Blood (Macbeth)* and *Ran (King Lear;* 1985). In all cases the action has been rethought in terms of Japanese history and Japanese society. And what could be more credibly Japanese than the end of *Throne of Blood*, in which Toshiro Mifune's bloody warlord is finally turned into an armoured porcupine with the arrows of his rebellious followers?

Whether Herzog is, as a film-maker, more masochistic towards himself or sadistic towards his casts and crews remains a matter of interpretation. Certainly *Aguirre*, an epic set and shot on the remote uplands of Peru, was as much of a trial as any of his films to make, and it was largely its international success which enabled him to make more. Klaus Kinski plays a megalomaniac conquistador in newly invaded South America, who takes off on his own and sets up an 'Empire of Eldorado', with himself as shield and defender – the wrath of God. By the end his whole army is destroyed by the climate, the terrain, and the poisoned arrows of the Indians. Even his daughter, with whom he intended to found a dynasty, is shot, and he is left alone, mad, on a raft of the dead. . . .

◁ NAPOLÉON (1926)
Dir. Abel Gance

Abel Gance's triple-screen epic on the early life of Napoléon has for long been accepted, mostly *in absentia*, as the masterpiece by which all other films had to be measured. In the fifties the first attempts to resuscitate it were made, but it came into its own again through the tireless work of archivist Kevin Brownlow in seeking out every surviving foot and restoring it to the print. This climaxed in the immensely successful London screening of 1981, with an original score, played live, by Carl Davis. A film full of amazing moments: Napoléon (Albert Dieudonné) on the field of Toulon is only one. *Photograph by Lipritzki*

△
WATERLOO (1970)
Dir. Sergei Bondarchuk

In Russia they call Bondarchuk 'the dinosaur', and affect to prefer the 1956 American/Italian version of *War and Peace*, directed by King Vidor at a mere 208 minutes, to his vast four-part fresco of 1967. That may be reasonable when it comes to comparing performances, but no one doubts that if it is battleground spectacle you want, Bondarchuk wins hands down. Not only in his *War and Peace*, but also in his subsequent reconstruction of the Battle of Waterloo, he managed to manoeuvre more people on to one screen, to more overwhelming effect, than anyone else. Well, with the whole Russian army at his disposal, what else would you expect? *Photograph by Paul Ronald*

DOCTOR ZHIVAGO (1965)
Dir. David Lean

David Lean and Robert Bolt, director and writer respectively, turned Boris Pasternak's great novel into a two-dimensional but visually impressive romantic panorama of the Russian Revolution. What most people remember, through the mists of twenty-odd years, is the endless repetition of Lara's theme on the sound-track, as a waltz, a march or an undifferentiated wash of swooning sound, and the vast expanses of central Russia, stood in for on this occasion by the rather more accessible (for Western film-makers) but slightly less expansive high plains of central Spain. Considering the size of the screen, it is amazing how potently it can be filled with very little: the snow, the sky, and one figure trudging into infinity.

INDEX